THE
REWARD
OF NOT KNOWING

—— *A Hero's Inward Journey* ——

ALEXANDER DEMETRIUS

BALBOA.
PRESS
A DIVISION OF HAY HOUSE

Edited by James D. Jackson

ISBN: 978-1-4525-5964-3 (sc)
ISBN: 978-1-4525-5965-0 (e)
ISBN: 978-1-4525-5966-7 (hc)
Library of Congress Control Number: 2012918211

Balboa Press books may be ordered through booksellers or by contacting:

Balboa Press
A Division of Hay House
1663 Liberty Drive
Bloomington, IN 47403
www.balboapress.com
1-(877) 407-4847

Because of the dynamic nature of the Internet, any web addresses or links contained in this book may have changed since publication and may no longer be valid. The views expressed in this work are solely those of the author and do not necessarily reflect the views of the publisher, and the publisher hereby disclaims any responsibility for them.

The author of this book does not dispense medical advice or prescribe the use of any technique as a form of treatment for physical, emotional, or medical problems without the advice of a physician, either directly or indirectly. The intent of the author is only to offer information of a general nature to help you in your quest for emotional and spiritual well-being. In the event you use any of the information in this book for yourself, which is your constitutional right, the author and the publisher assume no responsibility for your actions.

Any people depicted in stock imagery provided by Thinkstock are models, and such images are being used for illustrative purposes only.
Certain stock imagery © Thinkstock.

Printed in the United States of America
Balboa Press rev. date: 11/06/2012

INTRODUCTION:

The Reward of Not Knowing is an accounting of my response to the call of adventure. The very suspense of not knowing where the journey would lead became its own reward. Learning to honor life's mystery subsequently yielded its bounty. A shift in perception was the only requirement to unlock the blessings often found within tragedy.

My life was once a barren wasteland of an existence that played out between the regret of yesterday and the anticipation of tomorrow, turning the present moment into an unfathomable concept at which point enough was no longer enough. The need for excess increased as my compassion for others decreased. As a result, internal conflicts started to manifest within my body as tension and depression. Subsequently, anyone within my immediate vicinity also fell victim to that deadly influence.

So what exactly was that aforementioned wasteland? For me, it was living out an inauthentic life made evident by following other people's paths and resorting to animal-like behavior. No innovation or personal development ever took place along that way. Consequently, everything I truly wanted I didn't want due to the conflict between what I perceived to be attainable and what a mystical, inner-stillness, compelled me to achieve.

The Star Wars Trilogy served as a kind of guiding light amidst the darkness in my life. As such, Luke Skywalker's quest wasn't just some space-aged faerie tale because it followed three essential components inherent in most heroic fables; departure, initiation and return. Once Luke was displaced from his ordinary living conditions a pathway towards destiny was immediately presented to him. However, in order to fulfill that destiny he would need a useful tool of some kind (light saber), a long or short term goal (rescue the princess) and a mentor (Obi Wan Kenobi).

Learning to adopt an unorthodox approach to life transformed a nightmare into a heroic adventure. A departure from the realm of standard conditioning was prerequisite to the crossing of a threshold. Breaching that threshold was the key to an altogether new and rewarding perspective on life. Narrating my experiences to encourage and guide others toward a release from personal bondage becomes my final reward.

Bondage is a state of constraint by circumstance or obligation. In my own life, seeking freedom from this oppressive state was paramount. Years of enslavement to a mentally ill parent compelled me to seek answers in every possible direction. I have concluded through endless searching that the path to freedom is through an inward path. The journey unveils many truths about the seemingly chance events we encounter throughout our lives. If interpreted properly, these events reveal a pattern and can serve as guideposts toward a powerful transformation in each and every one of us.

In my personal experience, my degree of psychological bondage didn't become apparent to me until I left my mother behind. It is important to note that my experiences with her weren't entirely debilitating. Compared to the complaints of some whose lives I've encountered, my mom's condition was more a blessing than a curse. After all, she toughened me up and essentially honed the skills I would require to facilitate my own redemption.

Furthermore, I wasn't miraculously gifted with a heightened level of awareness. My need for answers evolved from an unbearable sense of anguish. Had my childhood been all fun and games, seeking a greater truth would not have felt so urgent. My mom truly loved all of her children. She just expressed it with her own unique capacity. And what is love but the pruning of the tree so that it may grow tall and strong.

My mother was the ringmaster of the spectacle that was my childhood. Afflicted by a mental illness called Dissociative Identity Disorder, her mind was divided into several distinct personalities inhabiting a single body. Because little was known about this disorder during my childhood, a life that could have grown into its own uniqueness was instead molded to mirror hers.

She left home to escape the clutches of her own insane mother. I eventually forced myself to leave home to escape her. Both of us severely beaten as children, our mothers were our chief tormentors. Hence, we built our own prison and existed in a state of schizophrenia. Both guards and prisoners, we no longer had, having lost touch with reality, the capacity to leave our prison, or to even see it as imprisonment. The unfortunate circumstance in which I found myself, however, yielded the opportunity to grow up playing a dual role, both as parent to my own mother as well as her therapist.

By the age of ten I learned hypnosis in an early attempt to root out her affliction. Her more oppressive personalities fed on both fear and hatred but once their appetites were satisfied they would lay low until it became time to feed again. I routinely conducted therapy sessions at home with a patient who occasionally, when she was able, doubled as my caregiver. Most often it was incumbent on me to assume the parental role. It was a classic case of the blind leading the blind. Still, within the darkness awaited the light. I needed only to be turned toward it.

My mother was the first person to open me to the mystique of the cinematic arts. Every time the credits started to roll she would ask what I thought to be the message of the film. From then on I perceived movies as more than just entertainment. Star Wars would become one of the first films to challenge my notion of conventional wisdom. The themes unfolded in that intergalactic saga closely mirrored the events of my own storyline. Perhaps I might yet witness the forces of light in my mom prevail over her dark side. Until then I eagerly absorbed all the cinema had to teach as well.

Movies continue to calibrate my moral compass. Most of my informal education came from either watching television shows or sitting in dimly lit theaters. As I initially fumbled through the many stages of life, the cinema helped me to deal with the challenges frequently encountered along the way. Thankfully, my mother never stopped encouraging me to glean the messages and life lessons inscribed among the flickering frames.

Consider how the politics of fear can enslave a society. Modern mythologies or movies dispel such fears when their messages convey a sense of fellowship between us and our environment as well as with one another. But a person or nation devoid of such a bond would inevitably foster the emergence of several distinct mindsets or groups that develop as a result of a general distrust of others. Rather than seeing one another as parts of a single organism, the opposite perception takes over. Every man for himself.

All organisms instinctively fight for their own survival, especially at the biological level. Take cancer cells for example. These deadly cells divide exponentially in their host organism. In a sense, these growths are willingly contributing to their own demise. The cancerous cells can no longer sustain themselves once they have destroyed their host. In killing their host, they kill themselves.

The current human condition can be perceived in such a way. Failing to recognize our relationship to the environment has led to the over-consumption of Earth's natural resources. The Native Americans had a living relationship with their environment. Everything from the ground up was considered sacred to them. Because their myths supported this belief system the natives acted to preserve and restore everything that was consumed. However, following the industrial revolution, the human relationship with the Earth turned into one of exploitation. When generating wealth became the overall goal of society the environment suffered. In turn, society's greed will inevitably contribute to its own demise.

Whenever my mother was lucid, her more compassionate and insightful personality took over. Since my relationship to her was always harmonious, these moments gave me the chance to learn all she had to share. She often used parables to illustrate certain conclusions. For example, I was told the story of a young man who desperately needed transportation so he attended church regularly to pray for a VW Beetle. He figured that his prayer request should be expedited by asking God for something modest. But he became increasingly agitated as weeks of unanswered prayers passed by. He couldn't help but wonder what the delay could be. After all, he was only asking for just enough to get by.

One day an old man from the church got wind of the young man's situation. Since the gentleman felt he had become too old to drive, he willingly offered the young man his practically new Cadillac. Yet the young man refused the offer as he was certain that the old man was up to no good. Besides, he still felt his prayers would soon be answered. The following Sunday, the young man finally heard the voice of God calling to him saying, "I wanted to give you a Cadillac but you insisted on a Beetle!"

My mom wanted me to understand that anything I receive in this life will always match my level of worthiness for it. She also wanted me to recognize that opportunities can manifest in many different forms. Therefore, it would behoove me to be alert for the opportunities that might lie hidden within any problem. Finally, she added, "Gladly accept whatever comes into your path. For what else could best suit your needs?"

Growing up, I was taught to keep my friends close and my enemies closer. If I kept an open mind they could teach me plenty. My own mother was paradoxically my closest enemy and thus a potent ally in my quest for personal understanding. Nevertheless, endeavoring not to disturb her fiercest personalities had me walking on egg shells for years. Yet when she would experience occasional moments of clarity there was no one else I'd rather have at my side. All the while, the abused child within her remained cleverly concealed behind an array of personas.

In her own search for answers she turned to an eclectic variety of ideologies. The range spanned from Catholicism to Spiritualism. Yielding to a single religion proved challenging for her so she skimmed a little wisdom from each. She concluded that religions are symbolic of an inward truth, not an external reality. They aren't the destination but merely signposts pointing the way. Similarly, growing up with my mother was a mere prelude to the greater odyssey my life would become.

The impulse to discover my niche in the world eventually prompted me on my quest. As with any ambitious endeavor, a departure into unfamiliar territory is the first step. Freeing myself from the insanity at home required me to discover my own path, venturing into the dark forests of self discovery. These trials and tribulations would ultimately lead to my rebirth as a self-directing adult.

Over the years, a legion of people confided in me while seeking my advice. A friend even confessed that my company was so therapeutic I should be available with a doctor's prescription. Many openly shared intimate details of their lives and their innermost secrets without my ever inquiring. Perhaps all they needed was a captive audience to hear them out. I could not help but feel that serving as my mother's therapist prepared me for such interactions. Thus, continuing to give of myself in this capacity might unlock further illuminations that could ultimately do good in the world.

Psychologist Carl Jung recognized that people around the world share the same primitive insights that transcend language and geography. He called them archetypes of the unconscious. According to Jung, humans are universally motivated by the same basic hopes and fears. He concluded that every human inherits these motivations from the same source. At one time or another, intuition likely calls upon each of us to champion a quest. Accepting or rejecting this inner calling remains one's personal responsibility.

While the quest that lies ahead of me remains uncertain, authoring a book feels like the first step toward unveiling something new and wondrous within myself. Perhaps the best way to be of service to others requires reconciling myself to an inward truth just as did Luke Skywalker. Through conquering his own fears and limitations he managed to restore balance to the galaxy. That was not his original intent, but a fortunate by-product of his success. Luke's quest awakened me to a profound realization. I had never realized the emptiness of my soul until it was revivified by the thirst for understanding through the adventure of self-discovery.

Scientists believe that at one time the entire Universe originated from a single source. If this is so then could it be that I am merely a thread of one enormous cloth, woven by single weaver? Since all things are inextricably intertwined, am I harming myself by doing harm to others? The only way to explore this concept was to plunge into the mystery of my own existence.

Everything in life carries risk along with it. The idea isn't to avoid all the obstacles on the course but rather to assume the guise of the hero by gathering competence and skill from hardships. Even the humblest life forms ignore the odds of survival once their quest is underway. Consider how freshly hatched sea turtles head straight for the ocean despite the predators that await them by sky, land and sea. Something within them spurs their little bodies toward an unforeseeable destiny. Uninhibited by fear, they simply heed the call to action.

In my situation, growing up with an unstable parental figure conjured up plenty of motivation for leaving town. My tragic existence became more difficult to bear with each passing day. Apart from leaving all the strife behind I also wondered what I could amount to on my own. Learning to perceive setbacks as opportunities ultimately helped me to see the world as it is rather than how I thought it to be. A personal hero of mine, Joseph Campbell, was a teacher who advised his students to follow their bliss. According to Mr. Campbell, seeking that which evokes your greatest joy will open doors where none existed before.

I never imagined the dangers attendant to heeding this call to adventure. However, once the notion set in, it was as if I mystically activated a homing signal that attracted mentors onto my path. These guides initiated the necessary conditioning required for my expansion of consciousness. I amassed a slew of characters (including my own mother) to guide and mentor me on my way. I was also encouraged to act from a place of natural grace where magic was the rule rather than the exception. For example, my mother taught me to visualize favorable outcomes until they appeared. When I was a child, we didn't have carpet in our home for several years, so my mother had me paint the concrete floors in the exact shade I wanted the carpet to be. Sure enough, despite all our financial limitations, the right people who could facilitate our needs began showing up.

In my experience, failure to understand something resulted in fearing it. Take Algebra for example. At first, its alien complexity was very intimidating to me. The fear only subsided once I achieved, through titanic effort, a greater understanding of the basic principles. Much of my understanding of life came only with great effort. Extreme hardship forced Luke Skywalker to undertake a dangerous journey beyond the farthest reaches of the galaxy. In actuality, his quest to become a Jedi was an attempt to discover what was in fact much closer, dwelling within him since birth.

In early childhood I faced the choice to either continue living the nightmare or find my own way out. In the end, my escape was illuminated by my inward journey. If I couldn't find the answers within, they could not be found. Divinely inspired entities graced my path as friends, mentors and even employers. It is a privilege to share their wisdom as well as my personal observations and experiences with you. May the insights I gathered along the way prompt you on your own rewarding path toward self discovery.

While continuing along these pages take time to ponder your latent talents. What abilities do you possess that flow from you effortlessly? These gifts hold the key to unfolding your destiny.

Enlisting these abilities can set the stage for improving your life as well as the lives of others around you. Acting out of inspiration has given me a sense of certitude that isn't easily discouraged by temporary circumstances. I would encourage you to be courageous in all your endeavors. After all, courage is not the opposite of fear. Courage is moving forward in spite of your fear.

So can a hero save the world? For me the answer is, "Yes! Absolutely!" But salvation must begin by exploring, charting and enhancing one's own understanding of the inner dimension. Cinema reaffirms that everything in life emanates from within and is projected outward. In the end, every production is a reflection of the director's unique vision. Thus, what better time than now to direct the life you have always longed for. External (man-made) circumstances might presently be disrupting harmony in the world, but they are only transitory interferences which, like time itself, will pass. The Universe, of which you are an integral part, will always continue to unfold itself.

PART I

⧼⧽

Departure

Chapter I:

What's in a Name

My birth certificate displays the name, Alexander Demetrius Minharez; born to both Linda Oyervidez Johnson and Luis O. Minjarez. The spelling of my last name differing from that of my father's was no accident. The *j* was purposely replaced with an *h* to make a subtle distinction. It was my mother's way of dissociating me from his side of the family.

She had never wanted marriage or children. Her dream was to become a school teacher, build a house with a library and keep horses. Instead she opted to get married to escape the domestic violence she suffered at home at the hands of her own mother. Her first husband, Carlos, was a Special Education teacher who aspired to become an attorney. Though their marriage started out on a meager note, it was about to become far more fruitful.

My mother's parents were frugal and built up a large amount of savings. I do not refer to them as my grandparents because they died years before I ever got the chance to establish any sort of relationship. At any rate, after they passed, my mother, as their only child, inherited a large sum of money which she then used to purchase a few investment properties and put her husband through law school. He soon earned his law degree, enabling him to secure a respectable position with the U.S. Government. The couple then had two daughters and Carlos' work frequently involved overseas travel.

During a trip to Istanbul, Turkey, my mother was involved in a serious automobile accident so severe that she suffered memory loss. However, she did recall attending an extravagant ball hosted by some top military brass shortly before the accident. She also remembered seeing a woman flirting with her husband across the room later that evening. Infuriated, she stormed out after confronting them both. She got into her car and drove off. When she regained consciousness, she was in a hospital with no memory of the events leading to her admission.

During this period, the man who would become my father crossed paths with my mother. Luis was a musician who played the tenor sax in his own orchestra by night and wrote musical arrangements for other orchestras by day. Carlos hired Luis to restore my mother's confidence at the piano because the memory loss had negatively impacted her ability to play. However, she got the shock of her life when Carlos served her with divorce papers for allegedly having an affair with Luis. Having no memory of such behavior, she asked her attorney for advice. The lawyer advised her to marry Luis. This would at least make her appear to be in a stable relationship which would help her retain custody of her daughters.

Thus, with the advice of her trusted friend and attorney, she married Luis. She always maintained, however, that this decision was strictly business. Because she never referred to him by any other name than Luis, I simply followed suit. Even though he routinely insisted that I should call him *Dad*, I always reverted to Luis. After all, their marriage was primarily a business arrangement, nothing more than a means of generating capital to start a recording company down the road.

Musically speaking, my parents were an ideal match. My mom composed the songs and Luis wrote the arrangements. They even played with some of the biggest orchestras in Mexico City. Success was right at their doorstep but she maintains that my father's lack of vision was at the heart of their ultimate failure. But the truth was she was harboring a mental disorder and that, coupled with her memory loss, wreaked havoc on all of their endeavors.

Dissociative Identity Disorder (D.I.D.) became the fatal ingredient in the toxic cocktail that was their marriage. My mother constantly berated my father and he had no way of knowing why because she wasn't properly diagnosed until several years after their divorce. As a result, their musical career started to spiral downward.

Physical as well as verbal bouts frequently broke out between them and witnessing these fights wasn't exactly a day at the beach for a young kid. On one occasion my father arrived at our home where my mom stood, waiting anxiously, by the front door. As he approached, she pulled out a .45 caliber pistol, pointed it skyward and fired off one round. I distinctly remember seeing him run off into the night, never to return. Their divorce soon followed.

During the divorce proceedings the state assumed temporary custody of my older brother and me. We were placed in a children's shelter before transitioning over to foster care. The children's shelter became our temporary home while the courts launched a full investigation into our parents' private lives. The investigation would later help the courts decide which of them was better suited to raise us, but until then my brother and I had to tough it out in state custody.

As young boys, I don't think we really understood what those proceedings were all about. Regardless, we had no choice but to acquiesce to our new living arrangement. I estimate that neither one of us was older than seven at the time. The day we were taken into custody my brother was visibly upset, crying the entire time. Overcome with utter disbelief, I just sat quietly in a chair and can remember shedding only one tear. The fear of embarrassment from crying in front of everyone was trumped by a much stronger influence. I truly didn't want to disappoint my mother who had always stressed the importance of exhibiting self-control, regardless of the situation. So it happened that hiding emotion became my standard technique for masking disappointment. However, I would later discover that whatever is bottled inside must eventually escape.

The children's shelter wasn't as bad as I had originally thought. We were given decent meals, clothing and our own twin bed. Kids of all ages, races and backgrounds were all housed alongside us. The boys' quarters were arranged with a row of evenly spaced beds on each side of a large room equipped with one large bathroom. At one end of the room was a door that led into the central foyer and at the other end was a door that led to the outside communal area. The girls had the exact same arrangement with their quarters across the lobby.

I often recall an incident which took place in the shelter that seemed to set the tone for my life's journey. It occurred one evening following a pillow fight that broke out in the boys' wing. At first I wasn't keen on taking part in the civil unrest but after a little coaxing it was on! Overcome with exhilaration, I completely lost myself in the moment. That was until our assigned custodian came in and broke up the escapade.

Now for whatever reason he sent everyone back to bed except for me. After escorting me outside he said, "Out of everyone here I'm the most disappointed in you for taking part in all this!" His assertion absolutely devastated me particularly because I would have all night to think about it before finally falling to sleep. Why was this guy holding me to a higher standard than all the other boys?

While I may never know the answer to that question, he certainly wouldn't be the last to have high expectations of me. Over the course of my life a seemingly endless line of people continued to expect more from me than I ever did from myself. In retrospect, it seems as if these standards were intended to prepare me for a difficult road ahead and even though I have disappointed several people along the way, something truly mystical arose from this pattern. I started to feel as if these strangers saw something valuable within me that could only be revealed by digging deeper.

As the divorce proceedings ground on my brother and I were eventually moved into foster care. The children's shelter was just a temporary haven for us until the state could locate a decent foster home, but as anyone who has ever experienced foster care can attest, there are good foster parents and then there are the *others*. My brother and I were about to get a crash course in the dynamic of the *others*.

The first home in which we found ourselves was headed by a single mother of two teenage boys. In her presence they were perfect little angels but the moment she left for work the torment began. For whatever reason, both of them had an aversion to my brother and often subjected him to endless harassment. The treatment I received wasn't much better. While one of the brothers hardly noticed me the other one took far too much interest.

One's first sexual encounter can conjure up many pleasant memories despite any initial awkwardness. In my case, however, I've chosen to separate that first sexual experience into two distinct categories: willing and *other*. When I was in that first foster home no one had ever introduced me to the concept of inappropriate behavior. Even if someone had, whom would I tell? After all, these were the people who were now sheltering us so it seemed proper to be compliant. Having been raised in a home where dissent was forbidden reinforced this behavior. Besides, as numerous foster children can attest, it could have been much worse. As I chose to see it, my foster brother's behavior wasn't personally directed at me because he would have treated anyone who was as submissive as I once was the same way.

Regardless of the genesis of the treatment I received in that foster home, it likely fostered a debilitating character flaw within me - the reluctance or inability to speak up for myself. My foster brother's demand for secrecy and my compliance essentially stripped me of a voice, so as I continued to develop, countless others took advantage of me in one way or another. It was as if part of me never left that foster home. Consequently, whenever I felt I should stand up for myself, my reaction was often panic and distress.

Despite those ambiguous moments between us, my foster brother wasn't entirely rotten. Not to make light of the subject, he did teach me how to ride a bike. Sexual deviant or not, there was another side of our relationship. Like most of my accomplishments to date, learning to ride without training wheels was not without its frustrations. At first, I was perfectly content to leave the wheels on, but my foster brother wouldn't have it.

Leaving me no choice in the matter, he removed my training wheels and ordered me to start pedaling. Then, while jogging along side me, he gripped the seat post to steady the bike. The first few times he released me I went careening out of control. Still, failure wasn't an option, so he ordered me to get back up and try it over and over again. Sure enough, his persistence paid off. When he released my seat for the umpteenth time a steady calm washed over me and just like that the bike was holding steady. At last, training wheels were a thing of the past.

I might have remained angry at him for his unwarranted violations, but harboring such hatred would never allow the memory to fade. On the contrary, holding the anger within only served to keep the image vivid and intact. It may seem twisted, but I owe much to that foster brother. Because he never took no for an answer, in many ways, his determination pushed me past my internally set limits. Once the training wheels came off I had no choice but to succeed.

Today that evil foster brother represents a totally new and invigorating concept. He is emblematic of the revelation that every evil that life has sent my way was accompanied by the tools or the assistance to prevail. The trick is to recognize that good and evil have an inseparable partnership. Learning to appreciate the up side of every negative has made it possible for me to emerge triumphant from all of those subsequent trials. By rummaging through my past, I was able to reinterpret the many blessings that were once disguised as curses. You might say it's as easy as riding a bike; pull it off once and you'll never forget how to do it, ever.

Fortunately, my actual brother and I did not have to endure the abuse in that foster home for very long. The social worker assigned to our case found an opening at another foster home and even though we were displaced yet again, it was a huge relief to finally bid a less than fond adieu to that *other* foster family. To this day I have no idea why we were moved. It wasn't as if either one of us mentioned anything to Social Services. We didn't even reveal any of it to our own mother. Had she known there probably would have been two fewer foster brothers in the world today.

Before arriving at our new home, the social worker briefed us on our new foster parent. Her name was Gracie and she was a recent college graduate who lived alone. Not a lot to go on, but after meeting her for the first time nothing else really mattered. Gracie was warm and welcoming right from the start - a complete 180-degree turn from where we had been only a day before.

My brother and I were still in elementary school during the divorce proceedings and because we moved around so much, it wasn't uncommon for us to make friends and then quickly leave them behind. After awhile it was easier to not form attachments to anyone or anything. But Gracie was the exception to this rationale.

Gracie had a knack for making us feel adored. She always showered us with gifts during the holidays and hosted fantastic parties at her home for all of our new neighborhood friends. She even commemorated our birthdays together so that neither one of us felt less important than the other on that day. She would make one huge cake and inscribe both our names on it. We may have been the only brothers in the neighborhood who celebrated their birthdays twice a year. We didn't mind at all.

In the Christian belief the word *grace* is defined as the free and unmerited favor of God, as manifested in the salvation of sinners and the bestowal of blessings. As with Gracie, her favor and dedication became the saving *grace* which rescued my brother and me from the dark and perilous realm of *other*. I can't remember either of our foster brother's names. Yet the one name I will never forget is that of our beloved Gracie. Eventually the courts sided with our mom, marking the end of our journey with Gracie. Wherever you are, thank you Gracie!

Our father was awarded visitation rights on weekends but it was a privilege that came with a price. In the days leading up to our weekend getaways with Dad, our mom would constantly bombard us with guilt for wanting to visit "the man who left us with nothing." She also resented him for giving us spending money during those visits because every dime we ever earned from her was the result of hard labor. It wasn't as though I couldn't comprehend her frustration, but an easy twenty bucks was always a welcome sight.

Prior to any of these events, my life began to unfold in a house we called Seabrook. Our mom referenced all her properties by the streets where they were located. Seabrook was on Seabrook Drive. Anyway, following the final leg of the divorce, my brother and I were told that we were about to take up residence elsewhere and that our new home was already prepared. My mom called it Rice Road.

When we first arrived at Rice Road there stood before us four cinder block walls nestled on an acre of land. As she guided us through the ruins, I remember looking toward the ceiling and seeing only sky. The house (if you could call it that) had no roof. Our new home consisted only of four cinder block walls and a weather beaten concrete slab. Talk about a starter home. However, as our mom saw it, those four walls symbolized a new beginning that would take place in an unorthodox living arrangement.

Several contractors advised my mom to tear those four walls down because, in their professional opinion, they would never support a new roof. Nevertheless, she completely disregarded their safety concerns and proceeded to piece together her vision. Working with a limited budget, my mom had to rely on the best of the worst carpenters. In effect, Rice Road was literally built by day laborers and a few ex- felons. Still, our mom was inclined to overlook their checkered past as long as they were willing to work for next to nothing.

The foreman heading this motley crew was an alcoholic named Willy. He routinely showed up to the job site stone drunk but surprisingly functional. Willy told me that his uncles started giving him beer when he was just a kid. Getting him drunk was their idea of amusement. As a result, Willy became a full blown alcoholic before puberty.

Despite his obvious shortcomings, Willy was one of my first mentors. By following him around the job site I could familiarize myself with all the various tools. He even took time to explain how various building materials contributed to the overall strength of the house. I always got a kick out of watching this inebriated genius work his magic. After all, his expertise is what finally brought our house to life, especially considering he managed to outfit it with a new roof in but a few weeks time.

To this day, those four cinder block walls stand as mute testament to our mom's sheer determination and persistence. Calvin Coolidge once wrote, "Press on. Nothing can take the place of perseverance. Talent will not. Nothing is more common than unsuccessful men with talent. Genius will not. Unrewarded genius is almost a proverb. Education will not. The world is full of educated derelicts. Persistence and determination alone are omnipotent. This slogan Press On has solved and always will solve the problems of the human race."

In the story of Jonah and the Whale, Jonah is cast from a ship into the open sea where he is swallowed by a whale. Often, fear of the unknown is illustrated by using dark waters and beasts such as the whale to signify the daunting circumstances threatening our existence. Additionally, the sea serves as a metaphor for the vast, undifferentiated depths of the subconscious - a blank canvas if you will.

Jonah sits in the belly of the whale for three days and three nights, praying and giving thanks to God for saving him. After the third day, God tells the whale to release Jonah onto the shore. Similarly, our home on Rice Road was the belly of a metaphorical beast. Our family's journey into that vast darkness began the moment my mother decided to make a fresh start within those four walls. With little protection from the elements, we set up shop by placing our beds on the concrete slab and using spare sheets as partitions. If storms were imminent, one of our mother's friends would board us for a few days.

Burning the midnight oil was more than merely a figurative expression at Rice Road. In an effort to offset the construction cost, we sacrificed electricity for the first few months. We used kerosene lamps for light and a portable kerosene stove for cooking. While some people pay good money to experience the camping life; we had the same privilege out of necessity. Still, with no other alternatives it wasn't difficult to accept our living conditions, especially since our small world was governed by a leader who never asked for our input.

Prayer was a fundamental part of our daily routine. Before bedtime we would recite affirmations of gratitude for the little things that made our lives easier, such as the new roof overhead and running water. Simply put, affirmations are positive assertions and my brother and I were conditioned to recite them even under the direst of circumstances. That "glass half full" attitude has seen many doors open for us along the way.

Since construction had to be halted whenever funds ran dry, the carpentry skills I had picked up from Willy were regularly put to the test. In addition, my mother never interfered with my creative exploits because she could always use a free handyman around the house. Painting was an essential skill to hone because color schemes frequently varied to accommodate her personality shifts. Yet such erratic behavior was nothing out of the ordinary to us. I am quite sure the same could be said for those who work in mental hospitals.

Our mother came up with some creative measures to motivate her two young sons to pull their weight. A public housing project once stood on San Antonio's East side. The area surrounding that development was in a state of decay and Mom used that situation as an object lesson for us. To her, those projects represented a metaphor for the form of bondage we fall into when we lack the initiative to overcome our circumstances. She explained we would essentially be condemning ourselves to the oppression of poverty. We would have to accept whatever handouts were tossed our way. Becoming indebted to someone else, we would lose control of our own destinies.

She even contrived a situation to make her case by driving us to the projects and telling us to get out of the car so that we could introduce ourselves to the new neighbors. In a state of shock, neither my brother nor I budged from our seats. Seeing our dismayed confusion, she took a moment to emphasize that if we refused to pull our own weight we might soon find ourselves living in those very projects. Nothing else was said or needed to be said. She had made her point. Unfortunately, my brother eventually moved out to live with our father, leaving me to carry the physical and emotional load all by myself.

As the solitary son, fatigue soon got the better of me. My lack of optimism could have earned me another visit to the projects, but she decided to mix it up with another approach. She handed me a twig and told me to try to break it in half. When I did so, she explained that she too could easily be broken if the entire work load rested solely on her shoulders. She then asked me to gather several twigs so that I could attempt to break them in half as easily as I had broken one. My efforts were in vain because they just would not give. She assured me that by sticking together, wc too could become indestructible. Ironically, the lack of coordination among her various personas primarily produced destruction.

A large mirror once hung in our living room. Its frame was ornately fashioned out of teak, making it a genuine work of art. One day as my mom walked past it, as she had done countless times before, a mental switch flipped, compelling her to rush outside and return with an axe. She flung it toward the mirror with a massive force. The impact sent the mirror crashing to the floor. That's when she took the business end of her axe and chopped it into an unrecognizable pile of rubble. Still, it wasn't a total loss. Our heating system consisted of a fireplace and a Franklin stove, so the shattered wood fragments were put to good use. Waste not, want not.

In a poetic sense that teak frame lived many lives. Like an embryo, it began its existence as a seedling. Through watering and nourishment the seedling gave rise to a sapling. After growing for many years that sapling matured into a tree. Throughout its lifetime that tree weathered many storms until a lumberjack eventually came along and harvested it for timber. Once leveled to the ground, our tree began another journey toward its ultimate rebirth as finely crafted wood products in the skillful hands of master craftsmen.

But that already impressive odyssey took yet another turn when a crazy, axe-wielding woman suddenly chopped it to pieces. The remnants were then tossed into a fireplace where they underwent another transformation. The heat of the fire divided the wood into its constituent carbon, oxygen and hydrogen molecules and released them into the atmosphere. Many of those molecules joined others in the heavens to form rain which then fell to nourish new seedlings. So the circle continues...

Mirrors have given me yet another insight, teaching me to refrain from judging. A mirror just hangs there, silently reflecting the present moment. That insight helped reshape my notions of what good and evil truly are, a partnership designed to strengthen my overall constitution. Hence, I can willingly participate in the game of life without falling victim to it. Achieving a neutral, mirror-like perspective has allowed me to see life for what it truly is - a cosmic dance of push and pull. I prefer to leave the judging to the critics. If all the world is a stage, why not enjoy it for what it truly is, one big rehearsal. From this perspective I can watch the performance play out from the box seats.

I often have to remind myself to turn inward to precipitate change in the outside world. By attempting to alter external circumstances first, attention is diverted from the real source of the problem. The majority of my issues were simply the result of inner distortion. I have frequently witnessed my circumstances shift shortly after transforming a distorted inner perception. As within so without.

Darnell was one of several bullies at my middle school. Because I possessed the ferocity of a church mouse, I was often his target of choice. One day during class Darnell harassed me to no end. At one point, my fear suddenly turned to rage. Feeling a meltdown was imminent, I decided to leave the classroom to escape the problem. Unfortunately, that didn't make Darnell magically disappear. His relentless assaults inevitably continued.

As fate would have it, the hectic conditions at home were grooming me to deal with scenarios such as this. Coming up with a clever response as opposed to reacting with anger has consistently proven to be my most effective solution to resolving conflicts. Moreover, my scrawny body could never withstand a Darnell-sized beating, so one semester I approached him in the gym locker room. At that point my back was against the wall both literally and figuratively. Making a firm decision to confront the problem somehow blessed me with a sudden insight. Since Darnell took pride in his burliness and athleticism it only seemed reasonable to use that to my advantage.

As one of the big boys on campus, everyone either feared or respected him. I told him that beating me up couldn't possibly prove anything because, frankly, anybody could do it. I then countered him with an even more inspired idea. After all, nothing is more powerful than an idea whose time has come. I asked him if he would help me with some strength training just to level the playing field a bit, explaining to him it would be an honor to fight him as an equal. In an instant, Darnell completely changed his demeanor. Not only did my proposal stifle any further attacks, it also paved the way for what would soon follow. Later that year Darnell and I ended up on the basketball team and because we were united by a common purpose, our friendship flourished.

Darnell was just an opening act in a series of trials to come. Innovative thinking proved useful in bringing about peaceful resolutions later in life. Still, it wasn't enough just to be clever. My intuitive nature needed fine tuning. Fortunately, my mother fulfilled that task. Drastic fluctuations in her temperament had me walking on egg shells for years. In time however, that same stress helped to sharpen my intuition. Having a thumb on the pulse of the person across from you can really come in handy.

When I was a kid it was common for my mom to kick me out of the house on a semi-regular basis. Avoiding this situation was a challenge to my heightened sense of awareness. Unforeseeable personality switches could send her on the war path at any moment. Like most bullies, she would take her frustrations out on the little guy - me. Her reason for expelling me was always the same; I was my father's son. Pleading for mercy from the other side of the door never helped, so after the crying and hyperventilating subsided, I would take long walks around the neighborhood to help me regain my composure.

For whatever reason, our neighborhood was blessed with an abundance of churches. Thus, whenever I was excommunicated from the church of Mom, I could seek solace in a church of God. One church in particular was ideal for laying low for a while because I could hide from view between the two large air conditioning units located outside the back wall. I felt more at ease on the outside than with the congregation on the inside. Having to explain my situation to a stranger might also get my mom in trouble, making my situation far worse.

It is ironic how my mom taught me to pray in times of desperation. Perhaps she knew it would come in handy in combating her demons. My prayers were more like wishful thoughts. The really big wishes (like a cure for her mental disorder or striking it rich) seemed to always fall on deaf ears. Smaller wishes, on the other hand, typically got a faster response, re-admittance into her home, for example. Timing may have been more important than the prayers. My hours of wandering gave her ample time to settle back into a more stable persona, one that was willing to allow me back in.

Sentimental objects had very short shelf lives in our home. Wood was often a secondary source of heat because keepsakes were frequently tossed into the fireplace. Over the years, the fireplace consumed family photos, clothing and even gifts. One of the artifacts sacrificed to the flames was an old trunk that once belonged to my grandfather. My mom held onto it for years but finally felt inspired to let it go one summer. She often told me that he had a generous and somewhat passive nature about him. He was even known to give the shirt off his back in both a figurative and literal sense which was in stark contrast to his wife, Louise. Holding onto that trunk was her way of keeping the memory of his kindness alive. When he passed away, she let go of the trunk but held onto the ashes from his cremation so her sense of security could remain intact. She still wept uncontrollably while the trunk slowly reduced to ashes.

My mom always called him Pimpaux so I just followed suit without ever realizing that he was my mother's father. After all, I was only six or so when he passed. As it turned out, his name was Daniel. His most striking features were his large hands and the overall healthy physique that he somehow maintained without ever exercising in the nursing home. My mom credited that little miracle to our Basque ancestry. Though he was sparse with conversation, his singing was incessant. Every time we visited with him he was either singing or eating and my mom predicted that the day he refused to do both would be his last. As always her prediction was spot on. It was a bit ironic and yet somewhat poignant that he passed away on Father's Day. As my mom saw it, he was bestowed with the gift of ultimate freedom on a day which celebrates patriarchs.

Of the many personalities dwelling inside my mother, one in particular was extremely quiet and unassuming. When that persona manifested I could hardly tell that she was even there at all. Her calm demeanor was refreshing but it was also awkward for me, mostly because I was so accustomed to functioning within a turbulent environment. Regardless, her cameo appearances brought some relief from the chaos. My mom often wondered if that was her one true identity.

Her ultimate ambition was to achieve a total mental integration, a process of methodically sculpting her many personalities into a single identity. She believed that a successful integration might finally bring peace to her manic life. Strangely, the idea of a peaceful state of mind was just as distressing for her. After years of struggling with the disorder, the only life she was familiar with and became best suited for was one of constant instability. That fact leads me to suspect that she was intentionally hindering her own restoration. And why not? Ending the strife might also put an end to her sense of identity.

Nonetheless, countless attempts to expunge this hardship from our lives only led to more hardship. Somehow, it seemed as if we were both missing the mark entirely. Our lives were beautiful and wondrous one moment and then suddenly horrifying and tragic the next. Was life presenting us with opportunities for achieving personal growth or just slowly torturing us? A distant memory tends to lean me toward the more affirmative interpretation.

During one of the bitter winters we endured in Rice Road, my mom was finally able to save up enough money to buy a few electric blankets. They were a welcome luxury to me because, for once, I wouldn't have to wake at the crack of dawn just to stoke a fire so we could start our day. That alone was its own reward. Beforehand, you might say I was the pint-sized hero of the household in charge of providing heat for the family. I had to learn to wield an axe early in life. That chore also happened to be a great way to blow off heaps of frustration from the seemingly unfair circumstance into which I had been born.

Hours of splitting logs rapidly developed my strength and endurance. After all, the incentive to work through the cold and fatigue was to stay in my mom's good graces. The alternative was to freeze inside of those four cinder block walls or even worse, move to the projects. Because the wood had to stay dry in order to burn properly, I also had to stack loads of it indoors before the rains came. Still, I gladly took every opportunity to be creative by arranging the larger logs on the bottom while progressively stacking the smaller ones on top, making sure that every pile was neat and orderly. Keeping everything orderly gave me a sense of pride, superseding the notion of doing it simply because I had to. In fact, that creative spirit transformed countless chores into conquests. While other kids my age were playing with fire, I was learning how to tame it, a theme that continues to play out in my everyday life.

Chapter II:

Divided We Fall

If you've ever daydreamed or become completely engrossed in a project or event you have experienced a mild case of dissociation. What a person with D.I.D. or Dissociative Identity Disorder experiences on a daily basis is far more severe than just an afternoon stroll into the clouds. In fact, their dissociation from reality is often indefinite, which is why it is considered the Holy Grail of psychological conditions.

Back in 1957, a book came out that was loosely based on the life of a woman (Chris Costner Sizemore) who suffered from the disorder. A movie entitled *The Three Faces of Eve* later followed. At the time of its release, little was known about the disorder. Today there are only a handful of psychologists who specialize in the diagnosis and treatment of the disorder.

Imagine that a small crowd of people want to interact with you simultaneously. Now picture what that experience might be like if each of them were attempting to do so while crammed into a single body. That very scenario with my mother made it impossible to predict which personality would greet me when I returned home from day-to-day. Each of my mother's personalities has her own temperament and disposition. Some of the more hostile despots had me walking on egg shells as a child, which served to heighten my sense of situational hypersensitivity. Consequently, I became highly proficient at detecting the slightest changes in her emotional state.

Children are imagination powerhouses and the make-believe world can be an appealing escape, particularly for those who grow up around violence. A traumatic childhood is often the root cause of a personality split, especially if the event involved extreme, repetitive, physical, sexual, and/or emotional abuse. The alternate personalities that emerge serve as a coping mechanism to deal with a perceived threat.

The word "dissociative" is ascribed to the challenge of people plagued with this mental disorder. They lose the ability to keep pace with everyday reality and thus allow their consciousness to run on autopilot. In other words, the lights are on but no one is home. This is why most of them appear to be experiencing a schizophrenic break. The only reality that grounds them is the traumatic event or series of events that caused them to check out in the first place. In my mother's case, severe mental and physical abuse were responsible for her mental split. As a result, an assortment of personalities developed during her childhood that could withstand the abuse. Without even being aware of it, she could escape into a temporary state of obliviousness, only to resurface once the abuse had subsided.

In childhood, my mother suffered both physical and verbal abuse at the hands of her own mother, Louise. I was born several years after Louise's death so we never met. Nevertheless, her character was very much alive in her progeny. My mother essentially turned into a facsimile of her abuser. In her photographs, Louise appeared to be a short, stern, no-nonsense sort of woman. I was also told that she could project her voice over several blocks. Not bad for a little lady.

Louise was a vocal coach and piano teacher and as the story goes it was my grandfather who encouraged her to teach their daughter piano. From the time the lessons began it was apparent that my mother was a minor prodigy. She started playing at age five and was already teaching by age twelve. Unfortunately, jealousy got the best of Louise, ultimately leading to the conflict she waged against her own daughter.

If my mom ever missed a note during practice, Louise would pick her up and throw her against the wall or slam the keyboard lid shut on her fingers. My mother eventually etched a small hole into one of the keys that she continually had trouble finding with her pinky. Since it was forbidden for her to look at keyboard while playing, the hole she etched into the ivory key would make that elusive pinky note far easier to locate. This way she could keep both eyes glued to the sheet music.

In my mom's day the career options for girls fresh out of high school were limited to secretarial work, domestic labor or marriage. She opted for the latter because it seemed like the most sensible way to escape the violence taking place at home. Meanwhile, the alternate personalities that silently developed within her from childhood remained utterly unaware of the other personas occupying the same mental space.

These personalities all shared the same basic identity, that is to say each of them associated their mental image with Yolanda (my mother). The tricky part is that each personality is trapped, or rather stopped developing, at the age that corresponds with a specific traumatic event. A toddler personality was discovered by one of her psychologists, leading him to believe the abuse may have started as early as infancy. When the infant was at the helm, all of my mom's motor skills were reduced to the basics. The moment the toddler manifested, my fully grown mother would suddenly walk and talk like an infant.

Another personality manifested as a vibrant teenager with the tendency to be extremely chatty, to put it mildly. At one point in my mom's life she received multiple shock treatments in an attempt to cure her erratic behavior. Hence, a personality resides within her that perceives she is still receiving shock therapy against her will. That particular one was often the hardest to deal with. Once activated, my mom would relive the entire ordeal in vivid detail. The episode could even take several days to run its course before subsiding.

When a personality switch occurs, the prevailing persona sometimes comes and goes in a flash without anyone being aware of it happening. It took me several years before I could distinguish one from the other. Still, every personality got an opportunity to come out and play. Something seemingly innocuous could trigger a switch. Identifying those triggers became a handy resource in my attempt to prevent switches from occurring too frequently.

At one point, it appeared that my mom had at least eight different personalities, ranging from infant to fully developed adult. One such personality was entirely underdeveloped and lacked the ability to interact socially. It communicated through grunts and moans that sounded like protests of despair and anger. The psychologist who initially encountered this personality believed that it was the one who absorbed the majority of the brute punishment and suffering that was inflicted on her in early childhood.

Despite her condition, my mother still made every attempt to instill culture in her children. She always preached that experiencing poverty and being broke are two distinct realities. Poverty refers to the state in which refinement or quality are absent in something or someone. On the other hand, being broke merely refers to an insufficiency of financial means to thrive – an often transitory condition. Therefore, she believed that we did not have to lead an impoverished life simply because our income was severely limited. Besides, some people are so poor, all they have is money.

Maintaining steady employment was next to impossible for my mom, although it wasn't for lack of effort. She just couldn't help but vacillate among multiple states of consciousness. At one point she sold Kirby vacuum cleaners door-to-door. The job was commission-based but strict policies based the commission on the buyer's credit rating - the lower the customer's credit score, the lower her commission. So even if a customer, with a low credit rating, ended up paying cash for their Kirby the peddlers still earned the lower commission. Still, something was always better than nothing.

During this same period she began to undergo hypnosis treatments which appeared to be the only effective mode of treatment to curb the disturbances. Contrary to popular belief, hypnosis does not render the subject unconscious. Instead, their state of consciousness is brought to a level that is calm and susceptible to suggestion. Unfortunately, Medicaid would only pay for 3 sessions per month, a fraction of what she needed to keep her inner demons at bay. Her solution was to train me to perform the task, substituting for her psychiatrist. Subsequently, each time my mom underwent a hypnosis treatment she would memorize the steps that took her into that state of consciousness. She then turned around and walked me through the steps. By age ten or so I was already well on my way to becoming her very own in-house hypnotherapist.

Any room equipped with a couch or chair could double as my office. After making herself comfortable, either lying down or standing up, the session would begin with me instructing her to count down from one hundred to one while I sat nearby. Somehow, my puny voice sufficed to guide her into that ideal state of relaxation. Shortly thereafter, myriad voices would spring out of her, sometimes all at once. I would then conduct the session the way she had trained me. Afterwards, she would awaken with total clarity, blessing me with a brief break from the madness.

I often wondered if D.I.D. was, in fact, real. The DSM-IV or Diagnostic and Statistical Manual of Mental Disorders, 4th Edition, is a manual published by the American Psychiatric Association. It encompasses every known mental and health disorder, stats by gender and age at onset, as well as research concerning the best treatment approaches.

Symptoms of D.I.D. include:

- Depression
- Mood swings
- Suicidal tendencies
- Sleep disorders (insomnia, night terrors, and sleep walking)
- Anxiety, panic attacks, and phobias (flashbacks, reactions to stimuli or "trigger")
- Alcohol and drug abuse
- Compulsions and rituals

- Psychotic-like symptoms (including auditory and visual hallucinations)

- Eating disorders

Diagnosing someone with multiple personalities is a lengthy process because many of its symptoms are quite common among many allegedly normal people. Just because someone suffers from depression does not make them a prime candidate for multiple personalities. Multiples often have additional disorders compounding their diagnosis such as bi-polar disorder and panic attacks. The DSM-IV provides the following criteria to diagnose dissociative identity disorder:

1. Two or more distinct identities or personality states are present, each with its own relatively enduring pattern of perceiving, relating to and thinking about the environment and self.

2. At least two of these identities or personality states recurrently take control of the person's behavior.

3. The person has an inability to recall important personal information that is too extensive to be explained by ordinary forgetfulness.

4. The disturbance is not due to the direct physiological effects of a substance (such as blackouts or chaotic behavior during alcohol intoxication) or a general medical condition (such as complex partial seizures).

Statistically, only .01% to 1% of the population suffers from this disorder. However, the actual number could be as high as 7% because the condition is often undiagnosed. Celebrities are not exempt from D.I.D. Retired NFL star Herschel Walker struggled with the disorder for years. I watched an interview where Mr. Walker talked about how he enjoyed writing poetry. One day he was asked by his doctor to bring in some of his work. It was then pointed out that each piece varied from day to day, as though a different person wrote each poem. It was not until then that he realized he needed treatment. My mother had at least six different styles of calligraphy and just as many signatures, each corresponding with its respective personality.

There is no known cure for dissociative identity disorder, but there are effective forms of treatment. Hypnosis and psychotherapy have been known to be very effective, along with medication and movement therapy. There is almost no anti-psychotic my mother hasn't taken at one time or another. The list included Lithium, Lorazapam and many other mild anti psychotics, but hypnosis consistently proved to be the most effective form of treatment for her.

Any situation or circumstance resembling the original traumatic event can serve to trigger a personality switch. The mental images that a person with D.I.D. can perceive are often so vivid their awareness of external reality can be obscured entirely. They may even be unable to distinguish another person's face from that of a former assailant, causing them to lash out at an imaginary attacker who may in fact be a friend.

Predicting when a switch might occur was more than challenging for me. Throughout my childhood I kept a mental accounting of all her triggers and could match them with various people or circumstances. Also, a movie theater, restaurant or any public place could trigger a switch. Even something as innocuous as the color of the carpet in a room could set her off. Because the reactions were so severe, I was in a perpetual state of anxiety. That might explain why I was never comfortable at large public events, even if she wasn't with me.

Another symptom associated with the disorder is referred to as dissociative amnesia. Each of my mother's personalities has its own set of memories. When a switch occurs, the inbound personality has little or no memory of what the outbound one has just experienced. The suffering one can endure from experiencing that sort of confusion is almost unfathomable.

My mother told me of an event that occurred years before my birth where she was involved in a car accident in Istanbul, Turkey. The incident left her with no memory and no upper row of teeth. Dr. Schoenfeld of the University Health Science Center in San Antonio, Texas, used hypnosis to treat her memory loss. During each session he would attempt to figure out which personality was activated from her most recent switch. Once he was able to isolate the guilty party he could then put it to sleep so the most functional personality could return to consciousness.

As her therapy continued, certain parts of her memory would regularly resurface. These fragments gave her clues as to the origins of the Istanbul accident. One day, after a session with Dr. Schoenfeld, she made a very understated reference to the accident. Sparse with the details, she mentioned being trapped in the car when a fire broke out. That was all she was willing or able to reveal. The incident was never brought up again and I knew better than to probe further because the expression on her face that day was one of sheer horror.

I still don't know if there ever really was an accident in Istanbul, but she insists that she was left for dead beside a desert road. I have however, seen photos of her travels to Turkey as well as to other parts of Europe. Still, the details regarding the incident were apparently so vivid that she has never once changed her story. Furthermore, she has always contended that her ex-husband was behind the accident the entire time, stating that he actually confessed to being jealous of her.

To prove it, my mom managed to save an audio tape recording that would authenticate her assertion. I was told they routinely communicated with lengthy taped messages to one another when her husband was overseas. She refrained from playing it for me until she thought I was old enough to fully understand its content. Also, because her daughters (my half-sisters) favored their father, she realized they would never listen to anything that could potentially tarnish his image so I was the only one with whom she would share it. That recording would make me the only other living witness who could attest to the sort of man she claimed her ex-husband to be.

As the tape began to play, I heard the man admit to harboring an intensifying streak of jealousy toward my mom because she always came across as more intelligent and charismatic to all of his superiors. He also confessed to using those talents to advance his own career. The final blow was listening to him admit to getting her pregnant early on in their marriage to impede any chance of her achieving success without him. It was refreshing to hear evidence that proved she was not just conjuring up wild stories.

Unfortunately, I was still entangled in a horror story of my own. Suffering many senseless beatings at the hands of my mother was a lot to handle as a young boy. However, in my rebellious teen years I was able to work up enough nerve to confront her about it. Surprisingly, she was reduced to tears when confronted with her violent behavior toward me. In her mind no such beatings ever took place. She could only recall spanking me once for something that, even I knew, was completely justifiable. It was apparent that my accusation had reached the wrong personality. This was verified in one of our hypnosis sessions when one of her more menacing personalities claimed responsibility for the unwarranted attacks.

The assaults were perpetrated by a persona holding racist convictions toward Latinos, prejudices ingrained from an early age. Since my mother's side of the family descended from European ancestry, she was exposed only to the belief that Latinos and other non-Europeans were inferior. Apparently she had married her first husband, a man descended from Mexican ancestry, simply out of spite toward her family. Still, her act of defiance was not enough to dispel her deep-seated biases. Unbeknownst to her, a personality had already evolved that replicated her mother down to the last detail. Furthermore, it had a large appetite for conflict and capacity for cruelty, loving to stir up trouble with anyone resembling a Latino, her son included.

My mom used to recite a Spanish saying to me which roughly translates to, "A man will burn down his own house just to see his enemy's house burn." It was astounding for me to witness this proverb manifest itself in actual life. A similar kind of destructive pattern emerged as my mom sought to utilize me as a pawn in a demented war she waged against my dad following their divorce.

My father was granted visitation rights in the divorce, but only on weekends. Even though he always appeared to cherish this opportunity to spend time with his son, my mom constantly painted a skewed image of him, leveling a barrage of insulting allegations regarding his character. Guilt was her weapon of choice to prevent me from siding with him. In her eyes, spending time with the man who abandoned us would be no less than betrayal. Looking back on it now, my dad didn't abandon us, he ran for cover in self-preservation. I only wished he had taken me along.

The personality who hated Latinos naturally included my father who was born in Mexico. Despite his musical genius, that angry personality branded him, "A low, common Mexican." These negative images were instilled from an early age in my impressionable psyche. In essence, those hurtful attacks were symbolic of the sort of destruction she was willing to wreak on her own house just to destroy the enemy's.

Many of my friends were also young when their parents separated. The difference was that I never heard of either parent blaming their children for the divorce. Yet that was exactly the kind of rhetoric that was common in our home. My world was reduced to absolutes. I was either with my mother or against her. Favoring my father was simply not an option.

One incident that followed their divorce undoubtedly contributed to the underlying sense of fear that lingered inside of me for so long. One of my mother's chief complaints concerning my father was his inability to pay child support, either on time or at all for that matter. Therefore, she charged me with the task of hounding him for money. Failing to execute this order would have been interpreted as evidence of betrayal. Don't get me wrong, we definitely endured hardship on our limited household income, but some of the extremes she undertook to collect those payments were over the top.

One day she became exceptionally worked up over the subject of money, so she had me call my father to stress the severity of our financial predicament. After he went through his usual rant, blaming a lull in work for the halted payments, I just hung up the phone. My mother then grabbed a knife from a drawer and pointed the business end at her stomach. In a deranged tone, she threatened to stab herself if I couldn't convince him to send more money. I immediately called him up and began pleading for money in utter desperation. I'm almost certain that my torment was palpable to him as he listened to her screams in the background. Without hesitation, he agreed to send more money if it would put an end to her tirade. Yes, my mom's proverb really hit close to home. Except in this case her own son became a casualty in a failed attempt to destroy the enemy.

I began to wonder if our hypnosis sessions were actually exacerbating the severity of her dissociation. It was never my intention to become her therapist or counselor. What I wanted was a parental figure to look to for guidance, but that clearly was not an option. The dynamic between my mother and me was reversed. This life would have been a heavy burden for any child to bear, so it's not difficult to imagine why I had to make the rapid transition from boy to man. Only now, as an adult, I can't help but feel as if I'm still a little boy parading around in an adult body. Furthermore, I can't help but wonder if the dissociative disorder was passed down in my DNA. For that reason I have voluntarily opted out of conceiving any children of my own. Instead, I decided to become more of a force for the change I wish to see in the world.

Spending time in the children's shelter made me realize that several of those kids were basically abandoned by their parents for life. I've often wondered where they all ended up and if anyone ever looked after them once they outgrew the system. Then I became aware of the growing number of couples who spend loads of money on fertility treatments instead of using it to adopt a child. In no way am I condemning the spending habits of would-be parents. I have just decided to take a different approach to addressing the issue.

During my father's funeral, everyone in attendance was given a little card with a short prayer on it entitled, "Indian Prayer." It read, "Do not stand at my grave and weep, I am not there. I do not sleep. I am a thousand winds that blow. I am the diamond glint on snow. I am the sunlight on ripened grain. I am the gentle autumn rain. When you wake in morning hush, I am the swift uplifting rush of quiet birds in circling flight. I am the soft starlight at night. Do not stand at my grave and cry. I am not there. I did not die."

Those words gave me some reassurance that his legacy would live on through me. The tender moments I shared with him reignite his presence, not the blood that runs through my veins. Furthermore, because my mother managed to instill a sense of decency in me, even while in the throes of severe disturbance herself, then perhaps I too could leave behind a meaningful legacy without ever having to spread my seed. Considering the larger picture, I could easily conceive of adopting and/or mentoring children who need the help now rather than merely dispersing DNA to beget future generations. After all, ideas can never be extinguished and nothing is more powerful than an idea whose time has come.

CHAPTER III:

Under the Influence

In surfing, the term *catching waves* isn't entirely accurate. In reality the wave catches you, provided you're ready for it. I experienced a similar phenomenon when I watched a series of video interviews entitled, *The Power of Myth* with Joseph Campbell. What he conveyed through the world of mythology truly captured my imagination. I first became acquainted with these works at an early age when my mother borrowed the series from the public library. Her ongoing search for understanding thus played a role in reshaping the path of my own destiny.

Joseph John Campbell was born on March 26, 1904, in White Plains, New York. He came from what was then an upper middle class Roman Catholic family. As a child, Joseph's father took him to the American Museum of Natural History in New York where Native American artifacts were on exhibition. The American Indian mythology truly resonated with Joseph. He eventually became well versed in their culture, studying the commonalities with other global myths. Those common threads shifted his focus over to the study of the humanities.

Joseph Campbell graduated from the Canterbury School in New Milford Connecticut. Eventually, his college career shifted to Columbia University where he became an accomplished track and field athlete. As a university student, Joseph was one of the fastest half-mile runners in the world. On a similar note, I too was once a track and field athlete with one of the slowest half mile records in the world. With the development of stronger and faster kids in athletics today I'm almost certain that my record remains intact.

Until his travels to Europe Joseph was a practicing Catholic. However, a chance meeting with a man named Jiddu Krishnamurti changed all that. This encounter sparked Campbell's lifelong interest in Eastern Indian and Hindu teachings. He also picked up several languages along the way, including Japanese, in which he remained fluent until his death on October 31, 1987.

Joseph Campbell dedicated his life to the study of mythology. With an emphasis on the cycles of life (departure, initiation and return), he managed to draw parallels between vastly different races and religions. These commonalities illustrated that people from all walks of life throughout the world share the same hopes, fears, and desires. Myths clarify these sentiments through allegorical narratives about gods, demigods and legendary heroes.

During his travels abroad, Joseph accumulated a few key mentors; Carl Jung, Krishnamurti and Nietzsche. He gained an appreciation for modern artists such as Salvador Dali, whose creative works also highlighted mythological themes. Professor Campbell, as his students referred to him, taught Comparative

Mythology at Sarah Lawrence College for thirty-eight years. He later married one of his former students, Jean Erdman, a dancer-choreographer.

After retiring from teaching, Joseph recognized that the general American public was ill-informed about world mythology. He therefore dedicated the remainder of his life to lecturing on his favorite subject, making appearances on college campuses and radio programs throughout the U.S. Shortly before his death at the age of eighty-three, Joseph completed a series of interviews with Bill Moyer produced under the title, *The Power of Myth*. That series ignited my interest in the body of work produced by this passionate individual.

While teaching at Sarah Lawrence College, Joseph Campbell promoted a simple philosophy with his students, "Follow your bliss." His counsel encouraged students to allow their paths to unfold in the academic world as well as in life. He derived from his studies abroad that forsaking an authentic calling for the sole pursuit of money robs an individual of the opportunity to discover his or her inner calling. Alternatively, those following a true calling may run the risk of losing money, but they will never be separated from their bliss.

Joseph Campbell impacted the world with his first book, *The Hero with a Thousand Faces*. In it, Joseph describes the hero as the personification of a culture's mythology. Traditionally, the hero was often a warrior, symbolizing the ideals of courage and strength. Over time, heroes began popping up in many other capacities. Explorers such as Columbus portrayed the hero dynamic through the opening of new worlds. Philosophers such as Socrates became adventurers of the mind. Finally, artists and scientists create transformational ideas that continue to shape the world.

In the Power of Myth Series, Joseph acknowledges the existence of a symbiotic relationship between the Native American Indians and their environment. All life forms were considered sacred. The air, streams and forests were also thought to be extensions of a larger family unit. These natives had a true understanding of the dynamism of life and the cyclical nature of all things

One doesn't need to travel deep into a forest to behold the wisdom of Nature. The intelligence of its design is even evident in an ordinary house plant. Observing plants has taught me the importance of maintaining an alignment with the source of all energy. For instance, the sun is the primary source of energy for all vegetation, but when a plant is deprived of access to that vital source of life it must find a way toward it.

One afternoon I conducted a small experiment to illustrate this point. I took a plant with all its leaves leaning toward the sun and turned it so that they were pointed away from the light. After a brief period, all the leaves shifted back toward the light. It seemed as if some kind of intelligence guided them back toward their source of life-giving energy. This intelligence also appeared to be urging the grass to grow even though I would religiously mow it down every week. After countless assaults from the edge of a blade, one would think the grass would simply give up and stop growing altogether, but the life force within it seemed just as relentless.

Similarly, the human body is yet another testament to the intelligence of Nature's design. If left to my own devices, my heart would have stopped beating years ago. Fortunately, a force within me never forgets to keep precise rhythmic timing for each of my vital organs. Likewise, I have never had to consciously keep track of inflating and deflating my lungs. Even my hair never forgets to grow back, although I suspect many follicles are beginning to take a permanent leave of absence.

Imagine the number of Post-it® notes one would go through just to keep track of the multitude of functions at the cellular level. Yet somehow Nature's intelligence pulls through again and again and again. This force behind all life also appears to direct the stars in the Universe with equal precision. These miraculous demonstrations within both human and celestial bodies could not possibly be happenstance. Hence, if my intention were to achieve greater self-awareness, then aligning my actions with this source intelligence must somehow give me an advantage.

Thinking is like a form of creation and because I made a habit of meditating on the same old thoughts, my life experiences were rather stagnate. Moreover, growing up in a constant state of fear undoubtedly reduced my odds of achieving a sense of balance in life and made me susceptible to dysfunction. However, the inward journey I was to take would soon awaken my ability to alter and improve my circumstances.

A journey, whether inward or otherwise, follows a sequence of events that are essentially the same for any would-be hero. Mine would involve the departure from a parental figure who insisted on fostering an old set of debilitating beliefs. If I ever hoped to create a deeper, richer experience of my life, the dogmas that controlled me would either have to be shattered or revised considerably. Through an initiation process, the hero attempts to transcend his own knowledge and conditioning. This leg of my journey would prove to be one of the toughest. Old habits tend to die hard. If the hero achieves success, he or she can return from the adventure to share the boons of their accomplishments and enrich the lives of others. The truths I learned and share in this book were attained through personal experience, not hearsay. Sharing these insights will hopefully inspire the heroic spirit in others so that they too might attempt their own adventure and attain their own personal level of understanding.

I've had a tendency to be led astray by numerous dead-end jobs because my obsession with money often overshadowed the consequences. Take, for example, my uninspiring career as a restaurant manager. At a time when my innate talents desperately craved some serious honing, I found myself working just hard enough to avoid getting fired. One heartbreaking shift after another finally led me to the realization that the journey surely outweighs the destination. So if I truly detested the nature of the work, why continue doing it? With that key realization, I initiated the search for my own Holy Grail. This quest would not be a search for a material object. Rather, my personal grail was an empty space waiting to be filled, much like the mouth of a cup. As my goals got further and further out of reach I realized that the journey was the ultimate goal.

In a sense, a hero's legacy is defined by a willingness to sacrifice for a cause greater than their own self-interest. Still, conforming to external demands can easily discourage a would-be hero, diminishing the desire for further exploration. In my case, the longer I forsook the path of uncertainty, the stronger the devilish impulses grew within me. What is a devil but an angel tortured by unfulfilled desire. It became apparent that a hellish existence would prevail if I continued to ignore my personal call to adventure.

I once heard an analogy that compared a person to an orange. When pressure is applied to the outside of an orange, juice comes pouring out because that is what is inside. The analogy suggests that when life applies pressure to us, we can only reveal what is contained within us. That analogy helped me to ponder the characteristics I reveal when pressure has been applied.

Considering the number of jobs from which I have been fired, pressure didn't always bring out my best. Failing to seek out a meaningful career led me to fail in several dead-end jobs. I never quite understood how pressure could cripple me so easily. Pressure was never an issue when I dabbled in creative building projects or composed love letters late into the evening. To illustrate this point, I offer the following anecdote.

The home where I grew up was a haven for the creative spirit to blossom. Since it was situated on an acre of land, there was no end to the upkeep. Due to heavy rains, the driveway, in particular, needed constant reinforcement with gravel. While it would have been ideal to pave it with concrete, the costs were simply too high. With that option out of the picture, my mother resorted to filling it with scavenged road construction remnants.

She would offer nearby road crews the opportunity to offload their broken asphalt fragments onto our driveway for free. Her proposal was a win-win scenario because the road crew would acquire a convenient and accessible dump site while my mom garnered free filler for the driveway. Spreading the piles of broken asphalt was automatically relegated to me because there was no one else who could possibly pull it off. Imposing this arduous task on a very young boy might strike some as a form of child abuse but I was always an eager-to-please kind of kid and it was never a big deal to me.

Although the work was strenuous, the hours always flew by. Work was a kind of game to me, fortunately so since I was never offered a choice in the matter. I simply chose to view the entire experience as a voluntary act. That simple yet profound mental adjustment altered my perception of just about any assignment, no matter how menial or tedious. Having so adjusted my outlook, my attitude toward the work simply followed suit.

Every pile represented a challenge instead of a chore. After each pile was conquered, I would take a moment to reflect on my most recent accomplishment. That moment of self-satisfaction eventually gave way to an overwhelming sense of awe and with that sensation coursing through my veins, I felt I could accomplish anything.

After hours of laboriously laying each piece of asphalt into place, an idea suddenly popped into my head. If positioned properly, these fragments could double as building blocks. With an abundance of material at my disposal, there was no limit to what I could create. So began my hobby of constructing miniature buildings from leftover asphalt fragments. The models were only a few feet high but they could span as far and wide as my imagination would allow. Much like composing one of my love letters, the outcome was rarely factored into the equation. I simply started fitting one piece with another until a four-walled configuration appeared. The rest simply fell into place.

To add character to the foreground, I engineered little streams through or around the perimeter of these carefully crafted edifices. My water source was supplied by Mother Nature herself. During rainstorms, we often set out large pails to capture water to irrigate our indoor plants, so any left over water was fair game. Once a trench was excavated and the water applied, the suspended sediment would cloud my little streams. To counter this issue, I lined the stream beds with tiny river stones that served to filter and suppress the unsettled mire, leaving the stream crystal clear.

All passages, though murky at first, eventually clear up. My acute appreciation for the darkness has always led me to a deeper understanding. Settling the dirt in the stream was analogous to the settling of my own scattered thinking. When

I began creating my little streams, it was necessary to introduce elements into the project that could help clarify the darkness. Even inner demons can play a crucial role in one's ultimate success. From this perspective, darkness has a symbiotic or mutually beneficial relationship with the light. Both conditions constantly influence and clarify each other.

Working out of an inspired state is what continues to propel me through any form of rigorous work. Claiming no choice in the matter is essentially a false assumption. Every path has manifold choices. Even refusal to make a choice (in the hope that the problem will simply go away) is still a choice. On the other hand, making conscious choices allows the imagination the latitude to develop a viable solution to any problem. The key is to work with inspiration and let it run.

When I began writing this book, the premise was geared toward promoting global peace because it seemed as though more and more people were ready to embrace the concept. Then one day I came across a passage that altered that intention. The passage read, "Everything emanates from within." It then occurred to me that in order to successfully promote peace in the world, I must first incorporate it within myself. While pondering this insight, the notion of starting a revolution emerged. Only it wasn't a revolt targeted at any external entity. Perhaps turning the adventure inward might permit me to quell my own inner turmoil and allow me to see the world anew.

Surprisingly however, I began to question my own integrity. Was I really capable of promoting change from within? Do I love, or even respect, the person I've become? Why am I not already at peace with myself? Would seeking the answers to these questions render a greater appreciation for life all around? At this point, only one thing seemed certain. The desire to pursue this adventure might never come around again. If not now, when?

I used to dread being summoned for jury duty. That is until an attorney, of all people, shared a profound realization with the jurors. He said, "People don't see the world as it is, they see it as they are." The attorney went on to explain that every story has three sides: your side, their side and finally the truth. He insisted that every person's reality only represents a fraction of the whole picture. Therefore, when seeking justice, all three sides must be considered.

That attorney's point really hit home for me, especially since I rarely considered the view points of others. Failing to do so distracted me from seeing any reality other than my own. In retrospect, it really wasn't hard for me to see why. My mom created a world around me that was fashioned from absolutes. Everything was either her way or the highway. With no other models to learn from, I simply carried on the tradition. I resented anyone who didn't suffer the same setbacks. However, the insight I acquired in jury duty that day transformed the rock I had been under into a great big stepping stone.

According to Joseph Campbell, no hero has to brave an adventure alone. On the contrary, he proposed that anyone courageous enough to begin one will undoubtedly see doors open where none existed before, provided they are following a genuine calling. The hero may even feel as though he or she is receiving supernatural aid from unseen hands.

Clairvoyance is known as the extrasensory perception through which someone can gain information about an object, person or location by means other than the traditional human senses. On top of everything else, my mom happened to be a clairvoyant, which made keeping secrets from her a real challenge. When I was a kid, she would supplement her income by giving spiritual readings. Most of her clients focused their concerns on trivial pursuits, such as winning over an already hopeless romantic interest. As far as my mom was concerned, this was like being asked to deliver horse manure in the back seat of a Rolls Royce.

Though the majority of her clients were utterly impressed by the degree of accuracy in their readings, they rarely reflected that sentiment in their donations. Apparently, revealing too much, too soon, was bad for business so my mom began telling her clients exactly what they wanted to hear. Suddenly the money started rolling in. Even so, she couldn't stomach this level of deception for very long and routinely closed shop early. I'm not certain which of her personalities possessed the psychic ability. What I am certain of is that her gift was extremely accurate with everyone else but me.

When I asked her to explain this anomaly, she remarked that a mother will always have a personal bias toward her children that will affect the outcome of the reading. I was perfectly okay with that because, in a strange way, not knowing what the future held gave me some sense that I, not fate, had control over my life. By the same token, I felt that the less Mom knew about the path ahead of me the less she could interfere with it. Because of her neurosis, I had to approach each day with a certain degree of uncertainty anyway.

Though my mom conducted every client's session in strict confidence, there were occasions when she would share a small snippet of a person's experience with me if she believed there was a lesson that I could derive from it. Even so, she would never reveal the name of the client to whom the story pertained. However, she did share the intimate details of one session that took place years before I was born, but only to illustrate the level of accuracy for which her readings were known.

As the story goes, a woman was referred to my mother because she suspected her husband of cheating. My mom immediately sensed this woman's notion was correct, but there were a couple of other details she felt somewhat reluctant to divulge. Nevertheless, the client insisted on full disclosure, so my mom revealed that her husband enjoyed wearing women's clothing for his male lover and that this all took place in their home while she was away at work.

Naturally, the client went into a state of total shock and disbelief, so to validate her perception, my mom took the reading to another level. She instructed her client to return home early from work on a specific date and time. A couple of days later, her client returned to my mom with some compelling news. After arriving home at the specified time the client caught her husband wearing one of her dresses and he wasn't alone. His lover was, in fact, a man.

Another aspect of clairvoyance is referred to as medium-ship, which many believe to be a means of communication between our physical reality and the unseen world. This theory however, is not recognized by science. As a kid it was common to see my mother slip into a trance-like state which she could induce by reciting a lengthy prayer, usually in Spanish. Afterwards, I would hear distinct voices from her unlike any of her known personalities. This is referred to as channeling an entity and many of her clients frequented our house to receive messages from deceased loved ones.

Many of my mom's friends had no problem discussing their readings in front of me. Yet something that I frequently heard in these conversations totally baffled me. A few of her friends confessed to seeing my mother's face morph to resemble the person she happened to be channeling at the moment. Their testimonials left me with an overwhelming sense of curiosity and bewilderment, especially since none of them could quite put the experience into words. All they could say was that I would just have to see it for myself.

On a day like any other my mom slipped into trance following her usual preliminary prayer. I just happened to be seated in the same room when something I'll never forget transpired. Just reflecting on it still makes the hairs on the back of my neck stand on end. My mom was standing by a set of French doors in our living room when suddenly her body started to grow or rather extend vertically towards the ceiling, but her feet never left the ground. I have always known my mom to be roughly 5'5" in height, but in that brief instance she was suddenly standing well over six feet. I deduced that measurement by using the doorway where she stood as a reference point.

When the unexplainable growth spurt reached its peak, a deep and powerful voice emanated from her saying, "Now do you see?" With my jaw halfway to the floor, I just nodded affirmatively. All the while I must have had a kind of deer-in-the-headlights look on my face. How was this possible? Only her friends knew of my curiosity regarding the morphing phenomenon, or so I thought. Apparently, some intuitive being took it upon himself to satisfy my curiosity once and for all. I faintly remember something else being said, but my overwhelming shock and confusion obscured the memory. Just when I had become accustomed to hearing her channel various entities, the body morphing thing came along and blew my understanding of reality right out of the water. Finally, with the same grace with which it ascended, her body reverted to its normal height.

Since this supernatural event occurred before my run-in with drugs and alcohol, I can attest that it actually happened. It is a memory that will likely stay with me forever. Still, it's a riddle wrapped in a mystery inside an enigma. To put the event into practical terms, my mom offered me the following explanation. According to her, no physical growth actually took place. The entity merely used the ether surrounding her body to project a semblance of its former self into the room. The process can be likened to transmitting a TV signal over the air waves and into a receiver to unscramble the encoded images. Is that all?

Sunday church was a staple of my mother's spiritual diet that she simply couldn't live without. She grew up in the Nazarene Church but eventually denounced their teachings because her mother imposed them as if they were absolute truths. She decided it was best to expose me to the ideals of almost every religion so I could choose my own form of devotion.

We often attended a broad range of religious services, ranging from Baptist to Christian Science. While we never took full membership with any congregation, we frequented the Spiritualist Church the most. The service we attended was headed by Reverend Gary Schultz, a man of modest stature who spoke with a kind of old time, southern drawl. Think Truman Capote. As far as I was concerned, every service, regardless of religion, felt like the longest day of my life. The only segment of the Spiritualist Church service that I found remotely interesting was referred to as the reading portion during which Gary would use his medium-ship to recite messages from the spirit realm to various members of the congregation.

Gary would begin the segment by removing his wristwatch and placing it on the pulpit right next to him. He would then close his eyes and go into a trance-like state. After a moment or so he would point to a random member or visitor and ask, "May I come to you?" The question indicated that he had a message for that person. Although the individual could refuse the offer, they never did. Gary didn't recite messages for every congregate.

Whenever Gary started making his way down the front row in succession, it indicated that everyone in the pews would be called upon that day. Everyone, including myself, must have looked like anxious game show contestants as we waited to hear those five magical words: "May I come to you?" On the days when he selected people at random, it was not uncommon for my mother and me to be called upon. Sometimes my grandmother, who died many years before my birth, would send her regards or an anonymous spiritual guide would offer up some consoling advice to each of us.

Most of the messages addressed personal issues about which the recipient had been concerned earlier that week. This helped to convey the notion that a watchful presence was always nearby. Furthermore, it was not uncommon for a message to contain intimate details that only the recipient would know. I often thought of those messages as an opportunity to communicate with a dimension unaffected by time.

Gary once relayed the following message to me: "It will all come out in the wash." He clarified the message by saying, "Things will work out because everyone finds out the truth sooner or later so don't waste time worrying about it now." I was just a kid when he passed that message on to me, yet those words continue to reinforce my faith in the existence of supernatural guidance. In one of the *Power of Myth* interviews, Joseph Campbell brought up an incident in which a Catholic priest asked him if he believed in the existence of a personal God. Joseph simply replied, "No Father." Then the priest followed up by saying, "I don't suppose there's any way to prove by logic in the existence of a personal God." Joseph responded by saying, "If there were Father, what would be the value of faith?"

PART II

⚬

Crossing the Threshold

CHAPTER I:

Thoughts Are Things

Most people will have a short list of vocations in their lifetime, but that was never the case with me. Though a few of my ventures might be too humiliating to mention, the fact that I suffered such indignities somehow makes me smile. I guess that which does not kill you only makes you stranger. Nevertheless, some of the greatest professional flops of my lifetime forced me to renounce several futile perceptions.

I was once under the employ of an insurance company called USAA. Like most successful businesses, they required all of their new hires to undergo a mandatory orientation. Since its inception, USAA has been highly committed to providing their workforce with the most innovative training procedures to maintain an elevated level of service. Therefore, all employees must become competent in the arena of critical thinking. For example, the idea of balancing 16 nails on the head of a single nail might seem a bit absurd, but during my own orientation, that marvel was actually proven feasible.

Many of these critical thinking experiments required teamwork, so we had to be separated into several small groups. That nail-balancing act became one our first critical thinking challenges. Each of the groups was handed a square piece of 2"x4" lumber with a 3" nail driven into the center. We were also given sixteen additional 3" nails. The task was to balance all sixteen nails on the head of the one that was driven into the wood. Our hands and imaginations were the only tools permitted in this undertaking.

Each team began tossing ideas around their respective tables. After several failed attempts, someone from our table mustered up enough courage to ask for a clue. One of the facilitators gave everyone the following piece of advice: "Think interlocking." What seemed virtually impossible only moments prior was suddenly made clear. In almost no time one group after another solved the assignment. The experiment clearly demonstrated that a practical solution to any problem was indeed possible. The ideas that didn't quite pan out were merely viewed as opportunities to wander outside our traditional modes of thinking.

Another facet of my orientation involved watching a prerecorded lecture given by an older gentleman by the name of Ed Foreman who possessed a youthful and magnetic presence on stage. Ed was a former politician turned self-help guru who headed a personal empowerment program based out of Texas. His program featured various techniques for enhancing personal as well as professional performance.

Ed started out by posing a question to the audience. He asked, "Did you know that thoughts are things?" At that moment I looked around at all the other souls seated in the room. The expressions on their faces displayed a genuine lack of interest. Yet his question had me utterly intrigued. It also seemed as though everything he said somehow related to me.

The pivotal moment in the lecture came when Ed began to outline his hypothesis on thoughts. He explained that the thoughts we think create instantaneous actions. When performed repeatedly, those actions become habits. Incorporating those habits into your daily routine is what builds character. That character then becomes the essential building block of your destiny.

Next, Ed asked the entire audience to take out a lemon. Everybody in the audience appeared rather puzzled by his peculiar request, so he said, "Go on everyone take out your lemon!" He finally drove the point home by holding out an imaginary lemon in one hand. Along with the entire audience I got out my pretend lemon and held it firmly in one hand. He then asked us to carefully examine its outer surface.

In the midst of inspecting our produce, he instructed everyone to take out a knife, place the lemon on a cutting surface and slice it in half. He also proposed that we breathe in the citrusy smell as the juice flowed out from the inside. I must admit that acting out this scene made the experience all the more palpable. Without skipping a beat he said, "Now bite into it!" Everyone in the audience let out a disconcerted murmur. The idea alone was enough to make all of our faces pucker up.

Ed went on to explain that our reaction was derived from a mental image. The brain activated the salivary glands as a response to what it perceived to be real. Once the image in the mind became sufficiently vivid, the brain could no longer distinguish between the real and the imaginary. It didn't take any further demonstrations to see where he was going with this.

I finally understood how thoughts propelled us and our bodies into action. This shift of perception ignited my aspiration to make wiser decisions.

Ed also explained that decisions are based on the outcome of past choices. The more choices we make, the more outcomes we experience. We then garner the wisdom to make better decisions based upon the successes or failures resulting from a multitude of choices. Everything essentially boils down to choice. Even choosing not to make a choice is still a choice.

Throughout his lecture, Ed referenced several books. One was entitled, *The Power of Positive Thinking* by Dr. Norman Vincent Peale. Dr. Peale's approach to self-improvement was, "Change your thoughts; change your world." Never being much of an avid reader myself, I suddenly felt the need to get a copy of that book. As Ed continued with his lecture, I feverishly jotted down all the other book titles he referenced. One theme in particular emerged from the various sources. The only person who can initiate change in your life is you.

Ed moved on to profiling the origins of personal beliefs. Simply put, beliefs are formed from the thoughts we fixate on the most. He claimed that the average person thinks about sixty-thousand thoughts a day. Of those sixty-thousand, most are the same ones we thought about the day before. Just as an engine locks up by failing to replace the oil, so our thoughts set up when new ones are no longer being generated.

His lecture inspired me to reflect on a few significant events from my past and soon it became apparent why the same tragedies continued to reoccur. Most of my thoughts revolved around lack, resulting in acts of desperation. This obsessive behavior stifled my desire to take a proactive approach to anything. Moreover, when I was too young to legally obtain a job in the state of Texas, my desperation prompted me to resort to thievery just to get by. However, not all of my shoplifting exploits were motivated by survival.

In grade school, Transformers were the hottest item on the market, so they were naturally priced out of my range. So I devised a plan to make off with as many as possible from a local merchant. To be perfectly honest, it didn't take a genius to outwit store security in the early eighties. I became rather proficient at casing an entire store in a matter of minutes. While perusing the aisles, I would make a mental note of items to steal. Afterwards, I would approach a random checker and ask for two large brown paper bags. My line went a little something like, "Excuse me. I just bought some large items and the bag they were in tore. May I have a couple more so I can double-bag them this time?" As soon as the clerk handed over the bags I would quickly retreat into the aisles to begin my pre-rehearsed shopping spree. Once all the items were collected, I'd calmly walk out the front door.

Is it any wonder why I grew to believe the world owed me something? My mother's conditioning, though harsh, was making a young, responsible adult out of me. However, I was perpetuating a nasty habit that would eventually come back to haunt me. An author named Ralph Ransom wrote, "Before the reward there must be labor. You plant before you harvest. You sow in tears before you reap joy." In one way or another, those words would surely have their place in the reshaping of my character.

My mother may have been a bit crazy, but she certainly wasn't stupid. To keep tabs on me she insisted I earn my keep by performing chores around the house, such as, pruning trees, chopping wood, mowing the lawn and cleaning. But I wasn't at all interested in working for meager mommy wages, especially when stealing proved to yield the fastest and greatest reward. As such, my core notions concerning honest labor were supplemented with feelings of entitlement.

Due to the unpredictability of her personality switches, it was virtually impossible for my mom to maintain regular employment, that is, until she entered the world of pyramid schemes. Because these were commission-based jobs, she was at liberty to write her own schedule. Over the years she sold everything from vitamins to vacuum cleaners.

Most of her earnings went straight into the mortgage, so little was left over for luxuries such as entertainment or family vacations. Consequently, I spent much of my youth getting high, by climbing trees, that is. From that vantage point I was able to observe a small wonder that routinely played out among the branches. Whenever a mama bird returned to the nest with a haul of food, the chicks would lunge at her to consume their portion. Even if the fledglings outsized her, that poor mother remained steadfast until every last morsel was consumed, only to repeat the process all over again. That scene helped me to appreciate motherhood for what it truly is - a sacrifice.

Perhaps that instinct which prescribes the nature of sacrifice to every mama bird was still operating deep within my mother, despite her illness. That may explain why she refused to surrender me to the state, or even to my father for that matter. Conditioning me to take on enormous responsibility required the patience and perseverance of a loving and ruthless individual. This was the dichotomy of my mother - God and Satan neatly rolled into one.

Being raised with two seemingly contradictory dogmas gave me the opportunity to synthesize the best of both worlds. Considering the results made it easy to tell which slant had the most influence on me at any given moment. By analyzing these conclusions I could determine which behaviors to hold on to and which ones to throw out.

All wordsmiths have their humble beginnings. My interpretation of heaven was etching out love letters to fleeting romances in elementary school. These letters contained subtle implications engineered to win hearts. I even made sure to fold every one of them into an origami-like rectangular configuration. Passing these notes during class was the counterpart to today's SMS (Short Message Service). Unfortunately, several of my teachers took joy in intercepting these parcels only to read them aloud in front of the entire class. After suffering this humiliation on multiple occasions, I eventually wised up and turned to exchanging notes between passing periods. It wasn't long before the length of these letters increased tenfold.

It never took much effort for me to crank out multiple pages (front and back, mind you) of prose. Regardless, I was no exception to the axiom, "Nice guys finish last." The majority of girls back then (and since the dawn of man) were only interested in the proverbial bad boy. Even so, at this stage in my youth I wouldn't know what to do with a girl after winning her affection anyway. In my teens and early twenties I chose to hold down run-of-the-mill jobs solely to earn enough money for survival. Unfortunately, this lifestyle turned me into a drone of sorts. Then a sense of hopelessness began to enfold me and the simplest tasks appeared daunting.

Whenever my mom reached a saturation point with her neurosis she would take refuge in a private psychiatric facility. Then, after adhering to a strict regimen of various therapies, she would emerge a kinder, gentler version of the beast that entered only weeks prior. Though most patients were allowed to opt out of group therapy, none were ever exempted from receiving daily doses of narcotics.

Most of these facilities had lush gardens, private quarters and a menu rivaling that of just about any high end restaurant. After years of visiting my mother in these resort-like facilities, the thought of trying them out for myself seemed intriguing. Not only could I get relief from the daily challenge of dealing with her mental illness, perhaps she might feel that her condition finally pushed me to the brink. Besides, the job I had at the time came with medical insurance, so allocating the funds to conduct this little experiment wasn't even an issue, or so I thought.

I had picked up a thing or two from my mother over the years so getting myself admitted would also a breeze. When she first sought help for her illness not a lot was known about Dissociative Identity Disorder. Regardless, no facility would admit her without just cause, but if there's one thing my mom is good at, it's putting on a show. The psychiatrist who first interviewed her concluded that she was both intelligent and coherent. So he saw no need to admit her into a long-term treatment program. However, he would write her a prescription for a mild sedative. That's when she asked him, "Would it be okay if I took this medication in the presence of George Washington and Caesar? Her response obviously struck a nerve because he followed with, "You mean you actually see George Washington and Caesar?" She just nodded as though it wasn't anything out of the ordinary and said, "Yes, we talk almost every night by the fireplace." That small performance prompted the good doctor to begin the admitting process immediately.

In actuality, she drew that story right out of thin air. She came up with the George Washington reference from a framed dollar bill hanging on the wall behind the physician's desk.

The psychiatrist also happened to be sporting a Caesar hair cut. Once on the inside, a fellow patient instructed my mother that citing suicidal thoughts would have been equally effective for getting admitted. That would later become the reason I would cite for getting myself admitted to one of those extravagant treatment facilities.

Sometime after my twenty-second birthday I concluded that it was time to get some relief from all the madness. In a moment of spontaneity, I quit my job just days before the end of the month. Then the following morning I took a bus to one of the facilities that once treated my mother. After strolling through the front doors with a counterfeit look of dread on my face, I stopped at the front desk and asked to speak with one of the attending physicians. When the receptionist asked me to explain my request, I simply replied, "Because I'm thinking about killing myself!"

In reality, I was too unnerved to move out of my mom's house, much less kill myself, but they didn't need to know that. After a brief wait, a physician came out, escorted me into a private room and said, "I understand you are having suicidal thoughts." I just nodded but was then utterly dumbfounded when he asked, "How do you plan to kill yourself?" Of course! Who thinks about killing themselves without formulating a plan? The thought had never crossed my mind, so like Mom, I improvised. My eyes were drawn to the tie around his neck and the chair upon which he sat. With muffled excitement I blurted out, "Hang myself!" And I was in.

Without health insurance, they would have summarily tossed me into the public health system, but thanks to my mom, I knew that those facilities were to be avoided. Hardened criminals and the homeless alike plead insanity either to avoid prison or to get a decent meal with a warm bed for a spell. The rest of the patients with legitimate cases were usually assigned to fresh interns with little or no experience. But thanks to the insurance card I flashed early on, that wasn't to be my fate. The doctor transferred me to another top notch, private care facility because theirs was fully booked. Apparently someone forgot to illuminate the *No Vacancy* sign. He instructed me to sit tight and await the ambulance transfer. He assured me that the physicians at the other facility were among the best in their field. That might be true, but even highly trained professionals can sometimes overlook the obvious. Just ask the doctor who interviewed me.

What I asked next should have unraveled my entire plan. "Am I going to be billed for the ambulance ride?" Honestly, should anyone on the verge of hanging themselves be concerned with their finances? He just looked straight ahead and said, "No." When the ambulance arrived a nurse escorted me outside to hand me off to a paramedic. The one who signed for me would be my chaperone all the way to the next facility. As we sped off, I couldn't help but notice that the siren was silent. What is an ambulance ride without all the bells and whistles? I politely asked if they could at least flatter me. The paramedic seated in back with me made a signal to the driver and in an instant we were lighting up the roadway.

One of my mother's personalities thrived on being symptomatic of one thing or another just to get expert attention from anyone willing give it. Conversely, I was always willing put the needs of others ahead of my own. Perhaps others could sense my eagerness to please and thus felt uninhibited when divulging their most private problems to me. Even the paramedic who rode alongside me was no exception. Something about my face must say to people, "It's okay friend. I'm here for ya. Lay it on me!"

So my escort asked why I was headed to a rehabilitation center. After sharing a few bits and pieces of my story, he didn't think I fit the profile of a nut case. Yet somehow this total stranger felt the need to divulge his own disturbing secret. Wasn't I supposed to be the patient in this situation? Perhaps I would not be the only one checking in to the laughing academy this day.

When he began to talk, I just sat back, listened, and rolled with it. He started out by saying that his birthday was right around the corner and his wife of three years was due any day to give birth to their first child. To me his situation seemed to be cause for celebration, but he had something entirely different on his mind.

He acknowledged that he had a lot to be thankful for with a loving spouse and a child on the way. But lately he had felt compelled to escape into the wilderness and lay low for a while without telling anyone. After sharing his dubious plan, all he could say was, "I just don't think I can deal with the way my life is turning out." He admitted that the desperation building up inside wasn't allowing him to think clearly.

By the time he had finished baring his soul to me, we pulled into the driveway of the facility I would call home for the next few weeks. Half jokingly, I said, "Maybe we should check in together. I'm sure there's room for one more." He just laughed and said that he would figure it out somehow. Before exiting the vehicle, I felt I owed him a bit of level-headed advice. What I had to say wasn't anything radical, but it came from the heart.

I started out by saying that perhaps some time away was exactly what he needed, but the people who loved him deserved to know the truth. If they truly loved and supported him, they could find it within themselves to forgive him. His complexion seemed to change after I dished out my free advice. Just before exiting the vehicle, he thanked me and we exchanged a firm handshake. After handing me off to the duty nurse, he wished me the best of luck and headed back to the ambulance. What a ride it had been so far.

Once I was finally processed, the nurse led me to my room. On the way there a man in another ward (enclosed with thick, impenetrable glass) was banging wildly on the wall and screaming obscenities. The force with which his fists struck the glass sent shivers down my spine. If he and I were to ever cross paths in a dark alley it would likely be curtains for me. All I needed now was for the nurse to tell me this guy was going to be my bunk mate. Thankfully, she informed me that the side he was on was reserved for the severe cases. As luck would have it, I was only considered mildly neurotic.

The nurse took the time to formally introduce me to a few of the other tenants, including my new roommate. He was an older guy who once aspired to become a lightweight boxing champ, but chronic back pain and a few too many blows to the head put an end to that dream. Unlike me, he had actually attempted to commit suicide. Despite his problems, I was really glad to have him around. He was the first person on the inside who made me aware of how good I had it on the outside. Like the paramedic before him, he didn't believe I was the kind of guy who needed to be in rehab. Over the next few weeks we became thick as thieves.

The ward to which I was assigned had a total of six rooms with two patients per room. Any patients who were deemed uncooperative were sent to the ward with that unruly, glass banging, character. For the most part everyone was as mellow as I, if not more so. One patient claimed to be a playwright. How apropos! Although I don't recall her particular ailment, as I have subsequently learned, dabbling in the art of creative writing is enough to test anyone's sanity. Both she and my roommate were religious smokers. While I didn't smoke, it was always a pleasure to join them in the designated area outside. Outside, by the way, was a square cage made entirely of chain link fencing. Still, seeing the sun and clouds in the sky seemed far more invigorating than spending time inside with the troubled masses.

One such troubled individual appeared to be the victim of brutal beatings. When she was first admitted to the ward, the doctors could barely get more than two words out of her. She claimed during her first group therapy session that the bruises on her arms and face were the result of a gardening accident. Must have been one hell of a dangerous garden! She also had another peculiarity that would manifest itself just before bedtime. For whatever reason, she believed a cat was hiding somewhere in the ward. Every night Crazy Cat Woman (as I often referred to her) would begin a room-to-room search for the elusive kitty.

I probably secured my place in Hell for reinforcing her conviction of said cat, but my need for a little lighthearted entertainment was far too great to resist. When she initiated her nightly ritual, I would stand behind a pillar and "meow" out load. Naturally, this triggered a frenzy, putting her pursuit into overdrive mode. I eventually had to end my antics when CCW nearly knocked over a quadriplegic's wheel chair in her attempt to isolate the meowing. Fortunately, a staff member responded quickly and rescued the poor girl from certain disaster.

Paralyzed from the neck down, this girl lacked even the ability to speak. To compensate for the loss, her motorized wheel chair was outfitted with an electronic talking device much like Steven Hawking's. She activated it by setting her chin on a lever attached to a mechanical box that was also outfitted with a small screen. Moving the lever with her chin in precise increments would transmute the motions into words which scrolled across the screen.

Feeling overwhelming shame for my inexcusable behavior, I thought it only appropriate to get this girl's back story. One day I invited myself to sit at her side and strike up a conversation. I discovered that just because someone lacks the ability to speak doesn't mean they lack the desire to communicate. According to her story, she had been seeing a boy of whom her parents did not approve. Having special needs himself, he would frequently drop by in his specially equipped van to pick her up for a little one-on-one time. Being in her early twenties, the allure of sneaking off with a boy was irresistible. I also got the impression that the two of them engaged in sexual activity. The thought alone made me more appreciative of the fact that love always finds a way.

Unfortunately, her parents didn't see it her way. Their concerns for her safety superseded their daughter's hopes and desires. Since she was a child, they had always been the ones to determine what was best for her. Yet to this girl, experiencing romantic love made her feel normal for the first time in her life. She said her guy always looked adoringly at her but the only looks she ever got from her parents were those of pity. But in an attempt to drown out her whimsical ways they admitted her into the ward to begin a strict regimen of antidepressant medication.

As I had learned earlier in life, there are always three sides to every story and although she could never validate hers, it was no less compelling. Something truly profound was encapsulated in her story. No matter the severity of our limitations, life has a way of propelling each of us into positive action. It's as though life has no objective but to fulfill itself - damn the torpedoes. Her story truly made me appreciate the gifts life had bestowed upon me.

In that moment I became aware that my mother's destructive behavior was not a personal act against me. Anyone in my place would have surely suffered the same emotional trauma I felt so powerless to change. My mom always said she was never encouraged to follow her own path. If obedience was the only ideal her parents ever instilled in her, could it be that her mental illness was fueled by an inability to make conscientious choices? If that were the case, continuing to participate in more unconscious behavior would surely plunge me deeper into the insanity that was part of my pedigree.

Choosing to shed my victim status was the only part of my existence over which I could ever hope to gain control. During my hospital stay, I was given daily doses of Prozac, subjected to group therapy, and had my progress rated by a professionally trained psychiatrist. Yet for all of that, it took a wheelchair-bound mute girl to illuminate my path to personal freedom. I just needed to use my two very capable legs to walk away from it all.

Patients were always encouraged to dabble in arts and crafts projects as a way to ease the mind, so I thought I would try my hand at making a friendship bracelet. Several of my friends made bracelets for me back in middle school, yet I never had the time or inclination to return the favor. Frankly, it seemed like a tedious task and my unwillingness to learn didn't help. Only now I was confined to a psych ward with nothing but time on my hands. The staff even gave me easy-to-follow instructions for stringing the entire thing together.

Throughout this entire psychotic charade, one person remained my biggest supporter; JoAnn – my then girlfriend. Despite our turbulent past, we could always rely upon each other. The least I could do to commemorate my love and appreciation for her was to string together a piece of memorabilia. During the span of our relationship, JoAnn tolerated receiving several late-night harassing phone calls from my mother. She also endured some of my mother's racial tirades directed at her Tex-Mex heritage, especially when I couldn't find the nerve to take the phone from my mom and hang up.

When my mother was growing up in Texas she experienced racism from both the Latino and Anglo students at school. Her pale skin tone reflected her English roots and inflamed the Latinos. Some of her old high school friends told me that the Anglos of that time were less than friendly to Latinos. My mom said Latinos would often shield their tacos while they ate so the Anglos wouldn't ridicule their meal.

Adapting to new school environments was a routine occurrence during my stretch with children's shelters and foster homes. On my first day of school I might find myself eating alone for a short time, but before long several students would welcome me into the fold. However, in my mom's time Latinos had to endure their entire scholastic experience in segregated areas.

My mom also experienced racism from the Anglo side. She didn't have a firm grasp on the English language because Castilian Spanish was the only language spoken in her home. Yet despite her fair skin she was subjected to much of the same harassment experienced by the Latinos. And the racism didn't end at the school grounds. My grandmother was said to foster racist convictions regarding certain Latino ethnicities, Mexicans in particular, claiming their lineage to be inferior to her own Basque heritage.

So the Caucasians dismissed her because she couldn't speak English and the Latinos rejected her because she looked white. Then at home she was taught to view her European Spanish roots as superior to both the Anglos and Latinos. Over time, Texas

Latinos had synthesized the English and Spanish languages, calling it Tex-Mex. As one might guess, Grandmother also took issue with what she considered to be a bastardized language, deeming it inferior to Castilian Spanish. Anyone speaking it was considered garbage, or so my mom was taught.

According to one of my mother's psychologists, the Dissociative Identity Disorder was already in full swing during that period. He was able to approximate the start of the condition based on the age identity of her youngest personality, believed to be an infant. Because the infant experienced rejection from all sides, a personality was conceived to reject all others. Having learned of JoAnn's Tex-Mex background, it was only a matter of time before her bigoted personality would lash out.

Despite her irrational hatred directed at JoAnn, I was still the primary target of my mother's verbal assaults. My father had almost no formal education. Music was the only field in which he was an expert. He would often ask me to help him spell words that I considered elementary. While I never looked down on him for it, my mother's partisan personality saw it differently. Once a switch was triggered, it was almost impossible for her to distinguish me from my father and she would often refer to me as a "low common Mexican."

When JoAnn entered my life she had no way of knowing what was in store for her. Despite the strangeness in my background, she never stopped believing in me. That loyalty and devotion is why stringing that bracelet for her suddenly became so important to me. After committing a few hours to the project I concluded that her bracelet would be better suited as a key chain ornament. The longer I made the bracelet, the less pliable it became. It couldn't possibly feel comfortable wrapped around someone's wrist. Plan B consisted of fastening a key ring to one end of it. Voilà – a key chain!

The colors I selected for the weave were red, white and blue which were in no way chosen out of my sense of patriotism. They were merely random choices. So as to give this gift a unique and personal touch, I looked up the meanings associated with each color. In the spirit of creativity, I made each color signify the following: Red (The love I give is the love I get), white (Surrender to a higher calling) and blue (Truth above all else).

Bursting with excitement, I patiently awaited JoAnn's next visit. Seeing her light up like a pin ball machine when presented with my humble token of appreciation made the wait worthwhile. She made sure to mention how very proud of me she was, and not just because I could do arts and crafts with the craziest of them. Something new and invigorating about my demeanor was obvious to her.

Perhaps it was because I was holding my head higher than before, or maybe I came across as more energetic and focused. Then again, my psychiatrist did have the nurses pumping me full of Prozac daily. Who wouldn't feel peachier with the latest craze in prescription drugs coursing through their veins? As for the handcrafted gift that I made especially for her, she somehow preferred that I hold on to it myself. In the long run it would have a much deeper meaning for me than it ever could for her. It would commemorate the fact that I voluntarily committed myself to a psychiatric care facility. Why not have something to show for it? The keychain remains in my care.

After two weeks of counseling, prescription meds and all the snack packs I could eat, the time to fly over the coo coo's nest had finally arrived. During the course of my rehabilitation, one incident involving my roommate stood out above the rest. One day, while seated on the couch in the common area, I heard a thud followed by a shriek of pain. When I looked over in the direction of the ruckus, my roommate immediately came into view. He was sprawled out on his back and appeared to be in agonizing pain.

I immediately leapt over the couch and ran to his side. Along my way to render assistance, another peculiarity stood out to me. No one - no patient, no staff member - exhibited any sign that anything was out of the ordinary. Most of those who knew me growing up would say that I was never one to make a big fuss about most things. In fact, I made it a point to mind my own business. Experience taught me that speaking up brought unwanted attention and unwarranted abuse. Speaking out against any injustice, no matter how great or small, just wasn't my thing.

Yet witnessing the predicament of that poor soul on the floor somehow opened a door within me. Normally, a sense of embarrassment would have prevented me from speaking out, but what happened next surprised everyone, including me. I cried for help at the top of my lungs. All the embarrassment, fear and trepidation that had once shackled me instantly dropped away. I had no intention of letting up until my friend got proper attention. Then a very unfamiliar feeling washed over me; it was outrage. It had always been my experience to have others outraged with me, not the other way around.

When help finally arrived, one of the orderlies had to pry me from my friend's side so that a nurse could examine him further. For whatever reason, the thought of leaving his side was abhorrent to me. Despite my protests, the orderly restrained me until my roommate was whisked away. Afterwards, I returned to the couch, my face covered with dried tears. Then a startling realization dawned on me. It appeared that taking a genuine interest in the welfare of another somehow short-circuited my old conditioned behavior. In that brief moment I was one with my friend, suffering the same terrifying pain.

Later that day my designated psychiatrist paid me a visit to discuss the incident. His explanation for my sudden indignation was both surprising and utterly disappointing. According to the good doctor, my mood swing was the result of my nervous system responding to a recent dosage increase. He went on to explain that the gastrointestinal tract produces, stores and distributes a hormone called serotonin which is responsible for generating euphoria in the body. Depression occurs when serotonin levels decrease as we grow older. The drug I was given was intended to help the body produce more of the feel-good juice.

After giving me the lowdown on serotonin and scribbling something in my file, our session was over. The feeling he left me with was reminiscent of an incident that once occurred between my dad and me. I was all of about ten when my dad asked if I wanted a rabbit. Naturally, I was enthusiastic. What kid doesn't want a real bunny? He then took me for a drive into the countryside. We finally arrived at a small roadside store and I waited in the car while he went in to retrieve my new little friend.

Soon, he walked out with something wrapped in aluminum foil. When he handed me the mystery package I asked, "What's this?" He then tells me, "It's the rabbit you wanted!" Sure enough, wrapped inside the foil was a skinned and gutted rabbit carcass. That wasn't at all what I expected. The enthusiastic inflection he put on his original question led me to believe the bunny would be alive. Once the truth was clearly understood, my heart sank into my gut. Similarly, when the doctor presented his flat and sobering explanation of my life-changing revelation, that gut-wrenching feeling overtook me once more.

The doctor emphasized that continued use of the drug would be my only shot at defeating depression. Part of me thought he should have at least exhibited a little admiration for my uncharacteristically heroic act. After all, most of my quirky contemporaries had to be coaxed out of their shells during group sessions. Yet there I was slaying my dragons in a moment of total abandon. Tough crowd I guess. However, his assessment lacked credibility to me due to one minor detail. While dispensing his grim prognosis for my life, the good doctor rarely maintained eye contact with me. Over time I've learned to be wary of anyone who can't look me in the eye.

As a child, maintaining direct eye contact was beyond challenging. Someone once told me that the eyes are the windows to the soul; I didn't want to risk anyone spotting the trepidation and vulnerability in mine. Logic told me that if a few of my mother's personalities adroitly exploited those vulnerabilities, then what might a stranger do? So avoiding eye contact became one of my defenses against the threat of unwarranted attacks.

I eventually had an opportunity to see how this defense mechanism looked in another. Her name was Sweetie and we adopted her from the Humane Society. Of the many pets we garnered over the years, Sweetie was, for me at least, the most memorable. She was a medium-haired, white mutt with a notably sweet disposition. In fact, everything she did had air of sweetness to it - hence her name. Whenever it rained she would sit outside the sliding glass door with her ears drooping. With her coat drenched and ears pulled back she resembled a white sea lion. Her big brown eyes, pointed snout, black nostrils and long whiskers really pulled the image together.

Sweetie was already fully grown when she joined our pack. Yet the kennel had little background information on her. Nevertheless, we could easily tell she had a troubled past by her timid demeanor and the dread in her eyes. Coming home to Sweetie was always a delight. Every time Sweetie caught a glimpse of me walking up the driveway she would sprint at breakneck speed to get to my side. Our daily ritual consisted of plopping down together on the porch swing while I rocked us both to and fro. I would talk about my day while she draped her head over my thigh - she my confidant and I her adoring pillow.

I slowly began to recognize some of my own jittery quirks in Sweetie. Multiple personalities aside, my mother's tone was naturally loud and assertive which was often interpreted by others as threatening. Whenever Sweetie was in earshot of this vicious tonality her body would reflexively crouch and her eyes would drift toward the floor. Also, if anyone made a sudden movement with their hands, Sweetie would react as if bracing for an impact, then flee with her tail between her legs. This happened frequently, especially since my mother always gesticulated with her hands.

One could only imagine what Sweetie's living situation must have been before her adoption. The fear that was my constant companion was now embodied in my beloved pet. Perhaps that is why Sweetie and I became so tight - our response to an external threat was virtually identical.

Sweetie continues to inspire me from beyond that ultimate somewhere. Since she never managed to overcome her timidity reflex, I often undertake my own small acts of bravery in her memory, such as when I look someone directly in the eyes. It is said that what we intend will surely find its way back to us. One of my greatest goals was to acquire the ability to look directly into someone's eyes without turning away. Thanks to an observant college professor, I was finally able to do just that.

This particular professor once asked me to stay after class for a brief one-on-one meeting. He then highlighted a habit of mine that I had never thought anyone noticed. He noticed that throughout the semester I rarely made eye contact with him or anyone else. But instead of attempting to isolate the reason for my behavior he offered a quick-fix solution. He suggested that if I stared at someone's forehead while engaged in conversation they would have the impression that I was making eye contact with them. To prove his point, he told me that his eyes had been fixed on my forehead throughout our conversation. To be honest, I couldn't tell the difference. Later that day I decided to field test his "foresight" technique on a few unsuspecting students.

I must have stared at twenty-some foreheads that day and yet no one ever called me out for not looking them in the eyes. But would the professor's trick hold up in the real world? Surprisingly, my subterfuge was completely undetectable by even the most discerning individuals. Either that or no one had the nerve to ask why I kept staring at their forehead. All the same, my confidence grew exponentially. Soon, my big browns were gazing directly at their newly discovered target. Finally, maintaining eye contact was no longer an issue for me. This victory was one for the books.

A shift of focus was all it took to overcome a condition that had plagued me for years. If a seasoned physician can't look his own patient in the eyes, then how legitimate was his prognosis for me? Somehow I was expected to believe that a lifetime of self-medication was my ultimate solution to avoid depression. The way I see it, depression is a gift. It is the mind's way of letting us know how far off track we've wandered. Upon being dismissed from the ward, I vowed to follow my bliss and do so courageously.

Avoiding, or rather postponing, my first instinctive call to adventure is what ultimately threw me off course. From the outset, I was not entirely honest with the good doctor. Suicidal thoughts were alleged to be the cause of my depression. What that doctor couldn't have possibly known was that it was all an elaborate ruse to redirect my mother's guilt trips right back to her. Perhaps I should have taken another course of action, but sporting a T-shirt that read, "Mommy's Travel Agency. We Specialize in Guilt Trips," wasn't sufficient to convey the message. One of my mother's personalities succeeded in scaring the thought of ever leaving her right out of me. But because I couldn't inflict my hate on only one persona, retribution had to be exacted upon all of them.

Still, after my release from the psych ward, the world outside had a new and mysterious glow. Although it was short-lived, my mom finally cut me some slack. Unfortunately, what started out as an elaborate strategy to alter her behavior ended up costing me a bundle. According to the psych ward, they were never able to process an insurance claim on me. All benefits were canceled when I ended my employment. I was left with a hefty reminder that vengeance doesn't pay.

In spite of the financial pain, the experience was worth every cent. If life's lessons were going to make a lasting impression on me, they had to pack a really big punch. The same would later prove to be true during my short stint in college. When I earned a scholarship to the University of Texas, my grades plummeted like a kamikaze pilot. Being put on academic probation forced me to enroll in a junior college. Only this time I would be earning money for classes and books by working two part-time jobs. And wouldn't you know it, the deteriorating grade situation was straightened out practically overnight. It was as if the Universe had intended my collegiate experience to begin at the community college level all along.

Though I eventually gave up college to help out more at home, all of my efforts were not in vain. You might say I still had one final lesson plan to master before hitting the road. A professor of Sociology helped me to recognize a crucial distinction between guilt and shame. According to him, guilt is experienced when someone feels they have offended another, especially if the offended is regarded as a higher authority.

He claimed to have tested his hypothesis on a few unsuspecting students by tripping them at random during passing periods. In every case, the students were extremely peeved as they picked themselves up from the floor. Meanwhile, the professor would stand by his classroom door, absolutely expressionless. The moment the students realized a tenured professor was to blame, their entire demeanor changed. Every one of them offered an apology as if they were at fault.

Shame, on the other hand, was an entirely different matter. It is generally experienced when one regards his or her own performance as sub-par. In his view, shame was a virtuous quality, serving as a sort of internal meter to help us monitor, regulate, or adjust our behavior. In short, there's no shame in being ashamed.

He added that people tend to use personal beliefs to distinguish guilt from shame. The problem is that no one comes equipped with a fully developed set of personal convictions. In fact, most will merely adopt and pass along the ideals that were handed down to them. He concluded that each of us has an obligation to find our own "true north." Otherwise, others will determine our destinies for us.

His research methods may have been a bit unconventional, but they got the point across. I suddenly felt ashamed for wanting to repay the guilt inflicted by my mother. Now I had the opportunity to use my suffering as a mast rather than an anchor. It was apparent that her erratic and misguided methods would never deliver me from my bondage. After all, she was simply repeating the behaviors handed down from her own mother. But why should I continue to pass that torch?

When I turned twenty-one, San Antonio had somehow lost its luster to me. At one time I had been willing to follow the orthodox plan for raising a family and growing old in our hometown. I never had any real ambition to live beyond the familiar boundaries of the city, so a steady nine-to-five job would have sufficed to carry me into retirement. But one day I bumped into JoAnn and fell madly in love. Because she always spoke so passionately about her desires and ambitions, I was inspired to develop aspirations for myself.

JoAnn always talked about wanting to move to St. Louis with such resolute conviction because when she flew there to participate in a spelling bee, the city made quite an impression on her. As the story goes, the people were friendly, the skyline was remarkable and every place she visited was clean and orderly. As a Virgo, those qualities were pretty much her thing. Just the same, I couldn't help but be inspired by her enthusiasm.

Everything that once felt like a hopeless dream suddenly seemed possible, but in order to initiate my own journey, I would need to have a specific destination in mind. Only where would I go? Hollywood had always been on my radar. How could it not? It's the Mecca of the cinematic world of which I so desperately wanted to be a part. Just one thing stood between me and stardom – mother. Challenging her had never been my forte, but with JoAnn's help my desires ultimately prevailed.

So began my campaign to leave town, but to do so gracefully would require my mother's blessing, or so I believed. Yes, I was twenty-one and still seeking her approval on everything. Yet, despite the validity of the request, my mom simply would not acquiesce to the idea of allowing her son to leave town. In hindsight, she had a sound argument. Permitting her passive son to move away prematurely would be tantamount to sending a little lamb to live amongst the wolves. While she may have persuaded me to pull back on the reins temporarily, I never lost sight of the ultimate goal - departure. Importantly, being in a state of perpetual bliss with JoAnn stoked my courage.

Moving in with JoAnn turned out to be one of my first steps toward salvation. The home we shared provided a safe haven for us to challenge each other's personal limitations, encouraging our growth as individuals. Experiencing some extreme highs as well as a few severe lows also helped unlock deeper dimensions within each of us. Learning and fostering the art of compromise is what ultimately brought us closer together. It wasn't as though we didn't have our differences. We simply preferred to focus our energy on what kept us united.

Be that as it may, the elements binding our lives in harmony would inevitably set us apart. Though we loved the thought of leaving town, our trajectories for the future were completely different. She aspired to become an elementary school teacher in St. Louis and I wanted to move to Hollywood to try my hand at acting. In spite of that, the idea of separating was much more difficult to overcome. We were, after all, best friends. Even so, it would have been exponentially harder to merely exist when we both knew that realization of our dreams was only a short journey away.

This period in our lives had all the makings of a mythological adventure. The most crucial sequence in any story is the crossing of a threshold. Ending my employment with USAA to move to Los Angeles symbolized one such crossing. Once I assimilated the lessons gleaned from orientation, the stage was set for my departure. Even though JoAnn would be left behind, I would not have to explore those new territories alone. At this stage of the adventure a hero can anticipate the appearance of a mentor who will evoke his or her finest qualities. The job I was destined to leave provided the guidance that would inevitably help me along my way.

CHAPTER II:

Atonement with the Father

My personality was, at one time, an amalgam or collage reflecting the restrictions imposed upon me throughout the years by those to whom I was obligated in some way. Whenever anyone would tell me to just be myself, I had no way of knowing who that was. Many knew me as a patient individual, but that was merely the outward manifestation of my submissive temperament.

Perhaps being forced to submit to the demands of others was life's way of coaxing my true identity to the surface. To overcome that state of dependency I developed in adolescence, certain people needed to cross my path who could initiate a restoration of my psyche. As fate would have it, a formidable male figure would later overwhelm the meek characteristics I learned from my father by scaring them right out of me, while a gentle female entity would also help to counterbalance the ferocity I inherited from my mother's most aggressive personalities.

Before a hero can begin a journey he must make some kind of atonement with the father figure. In other words, I needed to confront and be initiated by whatever held the ultimate power in my life. This step would represent the center point of my journey. Everything preceding this moment led me to this place and all that followed would begin from here. That which I had to confront did not have to be a male, just someone or something with incredible power.

When it comes to father figures, I consider myself lucky enough to have had several. The two most important were my biological father and, of course, my mother who also played a fatherly role in my life. Both of them influenced my perceptions about life, yet their contributions differed greatly. My father was extremely passive while my mother was more aggressive.

The first dead body I ever saw was my father's at his wake, a two-day affair. As his body lay still in the coffin, I was compelled to touch his hand to feel for any trace of life, but it was cold and stiff. The body was cremated that evening. The following morning the ashes were placed in a small urn displayed atop a tall pedestal next to a framed photo of him. A live band was also set up in the funeral home featuring several musicians who had played in his orchestra at one time or another. This was indeed a pivotal scene because it reminded me that nothing in life is permanent.

While attending his funeral I learned a few things about him that I never knew before. For example, he was once a wrestler in Mexico who shielded his identity with an ornate, red mask covering his entire head. The moniker he earned from his fans was "The Red Threat." And when playing an orchestra gig, he was always punctual. After all, music was his life. The person reading his eulogy concluded by saying that Heaven needed one more saxophone player and decided to take my dad because he was one of the best.

I also got to meet his side of the family for the first time. The opportunity had never presented itself prior to the funeral because my mother didn't want me to associate with any of them. Unfortunately, when we finally did meet my father lay dying in his bedroom. I was at work just hours before when a coworker handed me the phone and said my sister was on the line. I thought my half-sister, from my mother's side, had somehow tracked me down. But the person on the line was one of my father's daughters whose existence had been unknown to me. She told me that our father was dying and wanted to see me before he passed.

I immediately drove to the address she gave me and was led straight to his room. At this point he could no longer speak. Had I arrived the day before we could have shared some final words because he was still able to communicate. However, my newly found sister had some trouble locating my workplace. Despite the poor timing, having the opportunity to spend those final moments with him was more than enough. The hospice nurse claimed he could still hear me, so I just talked to him about anything and everything that came to mind while holding one of his hands with both of mine. Standing so close to his bed, I could actually sense which breath was to become his last. When the nurse officially declared him dead she called the ambulance. After the paramedics placed him in a body bag, they placed him on a stretcher and wheeled him to the ambulance which drove him to the funeral home.

At the funeral I met cousins, aunts, uncles, and siblings that I never knew existed before. However, despite the blood relationship, we were in fact still strangers. Even though we all agreed to stay close after the funeral, neither side attempted to maintain that commitment. I have felt closer bonds with non-related families than with those of my own blood line. Nonetheless, the sister I had just met at least invited me to the little ceremony she devised for the spreading of our father's ashes. We rented a boat to cast them a few miles off the coast of Corpus Christi, Texas. Only his immediate family was aboard to say their final goodbyes. Once at the site, my sister opened a little plastic bag and poured all that remained of our father's body into the ocean. When the ashes were spread onto the surface of the water, they slowly sank and faded from sight. It was a profound experience to bear witness to the final stages of my father's existence on Earth. He went from being alive and barely breathing, to lying in a coffin, to being reduced to ashes, then finally returning to the ocean where all life on Earth is believed to have originated.

Because my mother was my primary influence in adolescence, it was difficult for me to distinguish the character traits I might have in common with my father, especially since our visits were invariably brief. I obviously inherited my soft-spoken nature from him because my mom was no shrinking violet. In fact, several members of his orchestra nicknamed him the cat because he was always so quiet and unassuming. However, when it came to leading that orchestra on stage, my father took on a far different persona, confident and proud. He especially loved sharing stupid jokes with the audience. After all, the only person he was trying to amuse was himself. With his tenor sax in hand, the rest of the world could fall to pieces for all he cared.

A few years after the funeral, I was given, in an abstract way, the opportunity to see a familiar side of his personality that resided in me. This realization came to me when I attended a seminar featuring Donald Trump as the guest speaker. It seemed like a good idea to record his speech to review at my leisure later on. When I played the tape some days later, someone in the background possessed my father's distinct laugh. I closed my eyes and pictured everyone who had been sitting around me, but no one stood out in my memory. Then suddenly the mysterious phantom who shared my father's unique trait was revealed to me in a flash of cognizance. I was that person in the background who was laughing just like my father. Yet this realization would have never occurred had I not been momentarily outside myself, so to speak. Though we were rarely in one another's presence, that unsophisticated laugh reassures me that a part of him had always been and always will be an intrinsic part of me.

Sadly, I harbored a great deal of anger toward my mother for denying me the opportunity to know him better before his passing. Regardless, she continued to stand by her rationale for keeping us apart. She claimed that he conducted his life according to a set of ideals that restricted him to a state poverty and she didn't want me to follow his example. Her aspirations for me were always great. When I was just a boy, she had me commit an affirmation to memory and frequently required me to recite it in front of her friends. It was as follows: "*Yo soy un medico con fama internacional.*" Those words always impressed everyone in the room but me because I had no idea what the words implied and my mother never offered a translation. It wasn't until high school that a Spanish teacher finally deciphered the phrase for me. All those years I was telling her friends that I was a medical surgeon with international fame.

According to my mom, reciting that affirmation would eventually impress my psyche with the notion that I could become internationally famous in a positive way. The profession through which I accomplished that fame was irrelevant because she couldn't care less if I turned out to be a doctor, lawyer or business titan. All that mattered was that my exploits earned me a successful spot on the international stage. Her ideals for right living were aimed more toward high society where my father's aspirations for me were fairly modest. He wanted me to enlist in the Army so I would have a steady, well paying job. Conversely, my mother encouraged me to take on more ambitious goals. She helped cultivate my creative nature by encouraging me to draw floor plans for an ultimate dream house on paper napkins. She also took me to fancy restaurants every once in a blue moon so that I could acquire a taste for "the good life."

The dynamic between my two father figures was clearly defined, as were their expectations for me. Yet there would come a day when I would have to break free of the negative aspects associated with their ambitions for me. On one hand, my father's timidity set a precedent for me that allowed so many people to take advantage of my kindness. My meekness, however, was merely a mask worn by the bold persona patiently waiting for its inevitable release.

But the rage I had inherited from my mother had not yet been tamed, so once my submissiveness reached its breaking point, the anger would take control and cause others to misunderstand me. Yet even that sort of setback would ultimately become an opportunity to transform raw passion into compassion. Fortunately, once a hero does manage to break free from what or who he regards as an ultimate authority, he become reborn, in a sense, as a self-directing, responsible adult. The trick is to want to break free. Fear of the unknown impeded my earlier attempts to set myself apart from my family's distorted hierarchy of values.

I once had a fear of clowns. My father used to get me into the circus for free because his orchestra was frequently hired to provide the music for the acts. Sitting me close to the orchestra pit also made it easier for him to keep tabs on my whereabouts. Unfortunately, I always dreaded the clown performances. The fact that so many could exit from one tiny car truly creeped me out. The worst part was watching them journey into the stands to give away balloons or play a prank on an unsuspecting audience member. It was enough to make me hide behind any random stranger just to avoid being chosen. What was it about those faces with their fixed, painted smiles that frightened me so much?

In mythology, clowns represent the trickster gods. By mocking the human form and turning every natural impulse into a sort of grotesque action, these trickster gods are speaking past the normal range of our experience, allowing a transcendent message to shine through. If they appeared instead as large, imposing figures, one would be left with that image and the reference would be negated. Clowns are essentially conveying the idea that you, as you know yourself, are not the final form of your character or development. But if that was so, what might I be concealing within my psyche that I had not inherited from my parents? The thought of finding out was more frightening than just staying put and doing nothing. Fortunately, I was born under a star that is synonymous with adventure.

Articles outlining the characteristics of those born under the sign of Sagittarius suggest that we are seekers of truth in all things. Regardless of astrological signage, I have concluded that everyone seeks truth in one form or another. Being born into a roller coaster existence made truth-seeking my only logical course to realize change in my turbulent circumstances. Even my eccentric mother acknowledged the importance of seeking truth by attempting to provide me with an unorthodox education.

She rationalized that raising her kids was akin to constructing a skyscraper. If the entire focus is put on the superstructure while neglecting the foundation, the building would undoubtedly collapse. She thus made it her primary goal to send me to Montessori School by postponing the completion of our home. Although my run with Montessori was cut short due to funding limitations, the experience remains one of my happiest memories to date.

The Montessori approach offers a broad vision of education as an aid to life. Montessori is designed to help children with the task of inner development as they mature from childhood to adulthood. It succeeds because it bases its principles on the natural development of the child. Its inherent flexibility permits the method to adapt to the needs of the individual, regardless of the level of ability, learning style, or social maturity.

Children's inherent love of learning is encouraged by giving them opportunities to engage in spontaneous, meaningful activities under the guidance of a trained adult. Through their work, the children develop concentration, motivation, persistence, and discipline. Within this framework, the children progress during the crucial years of development at their own pace and rhythm according to their individual capabilities.

While I was attending Montessori, my mom would cart me off to school in an old mail delivery truck. She was always "wheeling and dealing" (as she put it) with mechanics for cheap and reliable transportation. One of the many gems she acquired was a solid green mail delivery truck with a matte finish. The flat finish was the result of excess oxidation and zero car washes. We often referred to our vehicles as male or female, depending on their function. For example, trucks were regarded as male owing to their heftier workload capability. Conversely, my mom loved Cadillacs and always referred to them as female.

According to her father, cars were not for the working man. He considered them more of a liability than an asset because they served no utilitarian function.

However, that green mail truck impressed my mother as feminine in nature because it reflected her true character. Its primary function in life was to perform for the sake of the family. Everything else came second. Likewise, my mother wasn't in the least concerned with impressing strangers. Her goal was to raise her children to maturity; period. As such, she rarely wasted money on frivolities such as getting her nails and hair did. Instead, most of her hard-earned income was spent on plants, books and education for us kids.

Similarly, whatever that mail truck lacked in aesthetics it more than compensated for in reliability. At first, the thought of being dropped off at school in a boxy, green beast turned my stomach because I initially believed the other kids looked down on me for it. Yet none of my classmates ever gave me any grief about it. On the contrary, it was a rather unique experience for them to see that green mail truck pull up every morning, especially since none of their parents drove anything remotely similar. As classmates, we were more interested in one another than in the cars our parents drove.

One classmate in particular captivated me with her beauty right from the start. I still refer to that young vixen as my very first crush. When we met during recess it was truly love at first sight. For the life of me, I can't even recall her name. What I do remember is her long, silky blond hair and the sense of grief that overtook me whenever we parted ways. We were two star-crossed first-graders caught up in a whirlwind romance. I'm almost certain neither of us had any notion of what a boyfriend or girlfriend was. We just preferred each other's company over that of our other classmates.

I dare say that our relationship even bordered on the sadomasochistic side. We often sat on the playground beneath a grove of trees that scattered small, red beans all over the ground. She took delight in showing me how they could be made hot to the touch by rubbing them vigorously against the pavement. They definitely packed a lot of heat for being such little things. Yet the pleasure she derived from the experience suited me perfectly because I rather enjoyed being on the receiving end of the pain. As Bill Moyers said in an interview with Joseph Campbell on the topic of love, "We often hurt most the person we love and heal the hurt by the love that hurt."

Alas, due to recurring financial setbacks, my tender affair as well as the entire year I spent at Montessori had to come to an abrupt end. The remainder of my scholastic experience would take place in the public school system, a stark contrast from Montessori. Nonetheless, my mom's valiant effort to immerse me in the deep waters of higher learning (even if for a little while) provided a decent head start for the journey to come; discovering everything else was entirely up to me.

I've often wondered how to tell the difference between true desire (which can lead toward a rewarding life) and obsession; between reluctance brought on by fear and resistance brought on by honest disinterest; between what is really good for me and what isn't. The most difficult step toward unlocking the answers to those quandaries involved leaving the nest. What I would soon discover is that the insane tragedies of my childhood were leading toward the realization that everything does indeed happen for a reason. Moreover, since both of my parental figures represented polar opposite degrees of thought, it behooved me to strike a balance between the two extremes to ultimately achieve harmony in my life.

CHAPTER III:

Leaving the Nest

By age twenty-six, my life revolved around an over-possessive girlfriend, a psychotic mother and a dead-end job. In my hometown of San Antonio, acquiring a job with USAA meant having a job for life, so it only made sense for me to try and get one foot in the door. After three consecutive attempts, they finally offered me an entry level position as a Customer Service Representative, a glorified title for phone operator.

The job consisted primarily of transferring calls to their respective parties and since the majority of inbound calls involved pending insurance claims, I routinely became an easy target for a lot of unchecked aggression. Many of these irate callers failed to understand how powerless I was to help. These calls could have plagued me with frustration and anger, but I made the conscious decision to start listening with indifference.

Buddhism dictates that all life is sorrowful. However, a psychological indifference to suffering lifts the burden of sorrow. In a Zen story, the Buddha was delivering a sermon to his disciples while walking through a village. Out of nowhere, a stranger joined the group and began to taunt the Buddha. Yet, despite the barrage of foul remarks, the Buddha calmly continued his address. Once the group wandered beyond the village walls, the hostile stranger went on his way.

One disciple couldn't help but ask the Buddha, "How were you able to maintain your composure in the presence of such an annoyance?" He replied, "If someone gives you a gift and you do not accept the gift, to whom does the gift belong?" I've come to appreciate all the boorish souls who have crossed my path at one time or another. As I see it, they were divine gifts sent to challenge and strengthen my resolve. I could have either embraced them or sidestepped them. But why fight them?

Every act in life casts pairs of opposites. It's got to be that way to maintain balance in any scenario. Severe weather, for example, is created when cold air collides with warm air. The unstable air must reestablish equilibrium, giving rise to storms. These storms might be a nuisance for some, but to the planet they are an essential part of maintaining balance within the atmosphere.

As with love, my experience always felt more relevant when preceded by an extensive run-in with agony. Similarly, joy would seem meaningless without the experience of despair behind it. If everything in this world were green, we would never experience color. It seems that the dynamics of contrast are the very source of creativity. Therefore, I find it helpful to remember that both extremes add value to the experience of the whole. I've often heard people say, "Someday we're going to look back on this moment and laugh." Why delay the opportunity? Laugh now.

Before my departure from Texas, I was living with JoAnn. We had a relationship that ran hot and cold for nearly six years. Previously, my all-time record for maintaining a steady relationship was around two months. I met JoAnn while on a road trip to South Padre Island with my mother. Taking a lengthy road trip to vacation with my mom in a notorious party town wasn't the ideal scenario, but it presented an opportunity to get out of San Antonio, however briefly. Granted, my hometown was a great place to grow up but the thought of living there forever was not at all appealing.

When we finally arrived in Corpus Christi where we thought South Padre Island was located, we couldn't find our hotel. Since neither of us had ever been to South Padre Island, it was clear that the blind were leading the blind. As it turned out, I had misread the map entirely. This minor snafu had led us straight into the heart of Corpus Christi and onto South Padre Island Drive. When we stopped at a gas station to ask for directions, the attendant informed us that the actual town of South Padre Island was roughly two hours away.

Consider the word *lost* for a moment. It's defined as not knowing one's whereabouts. Often, the very condition of not knowing can lead to an adventure. For my adventure to unfold, life simply needed to detour me off the beaten path for a bit. To get reoriented, I pulled into the first hotel we spotted. Standing behind the front desk was one of the most beautiful girls I had ever set eyes on. Her name was JoAnn. Our interaction was rather brief since all we really needed were directions, but the enchantment of the chance meeting stayed with me for the remainder of the drive.

When we finally arrived in South Padre Island, our hotel wasn't exactly as depicted in the brochure. To make matters worse, the front desk placed us in a room overlooking the parking lot rather than the ocean view room we had reserved. This all started me thinking about JoAnn and how professional and sincere she came across with both my mother and me. Suddenly, Corpus Christi felt like the obvious destination choice. It didn't even take much effort to sway my mom. We simply loaded up the car and doubled back.

During our stay in Corpus, I routinely frequented the front desk where JoAnn held her post. Talking to her was so effortless that time seemed to stand still. I felt it would be a major mistake to not make an effort to stay in touch. On the day we were scheduled to check out, I wrote JoAnn a letter. The plan was to hand it to her while we were checking out, but to my dismay she was off that day. Nevertheless, the girl behind the desk assured me that JoAnn would get it, so my mom and I headed back to San Antonio.

Days later I got a call from a vaguely familiar area code. It was JoAnn. We talked for hours that day. As with all our subsequent conversations, there was never any real sense of time between us. Instead, it felt as if we experienced an eternity together in only a few brief moments. We even started exchanging written correspondence practically every day to avoid tying up the phone line. Each of those letters had an endearing quality that still surpasses all modern forms of communication.

JoAnn brought excitement into my tiny bubble of existence. Adding to her allure was the fact that a great distance separated the two of us. Corpus Christi is a two-and-a-half hour drive from San Antonio if one observes the posted limit. Before she entered my life, I had no incentive to travel beyond San Antonio, but love would indeed put an end to all of that. An even greater adventure would unfold when she decided to leave her hometown and move in with me. Inexperienced youth would become the driving force behind our partnership that would soon become a roller coaster ride of exhilarating highs and wrenching lows.

Speaking of which, I used to have a debilitating fear of roller coasters. Thankfully, JoAnn made my rehabilitation a fun and practical exercise that would push me past my old limits. Every year downtown San Antonio is host to a carnival featuring an assortment of thrilling rides and attractions. On one of those occasions, JoAnn persuaded me to ride a kiddy roller coaster as an intermediate step, but instead of joining me she just stood near the ride to observe my reactions.

Afterwards, JoAnn gave me her appraisal of the situation. According to her report, I began the ride with a sour grin on my face. That subtle factor helped her devise a strategy. She theorized that if I forced a smile as the ride began, the fear would eventually subside. Then, when the lead car makes its way over the peak, I should immediately convert that smile into a faint laugh. Combined with the adrenaline in my body, that bogus laugh should evolve into genuine euphoria as the ride continued to plummet down the line.

JoAnn also felt it appropriate to test her theory on some serious equipment. This sparked an impromptu road trip to Six Flags in Houston, home to one of the tallest wooden roller coasters in the world. The fear brewing inside me on the four-hour car ride was palpable. She was resolved that we weren't leaving until the beast was slain. Once at the park, we took a moment to stand at a distance from the ride. JoAnn couldn't resist pointing out that whole sections of the structure swayed back and forth as the cars sped along the tracks. If this was another test, I wasn't flinching. We hadn't come all this way to turn back now.

As we sat in our seats awaiting the moment of truth, I took the added precaution of jamming the support bar as close to my thighs as humanly possible. Safety first. When the buzzer sounded we were on our way and beyond the point of no return. Remembering JoAnn's proposal, I fabricated a cheesy smile that steadily morphed into nervous laughter as we clicked and clacked our way to the tippy top. The view from that height was utterly breathtaking, but the real thrill was still to come.

The first drop felt more like a free fall. Even though my jaw dropped to the floor I was experiencing a sort of jubilant hysteria. I could feel all that nervous energy rushing through me, only this time it didn't manifest itself as fear. Instead it felt as if a heavy dose of euphoria was coursing through my veins. The adrenaline must have amplified the sensations I attempted to express at the beginning of the ride because what had been so debilitating only hours before was now experienced as bliss. JoAnn's desire to see me succeed coupled with her innovative idea helped me overcome yet another obstacle.

On the opposite end of the spectrum was my mother who, in conjunction with her dissociative condition, routinely wreaked havoc on the lives of everyone around her. It was only a matter of time before this disturbance would spill over into my relationship with JoAnn. Yet, despite having had no prior experience with mental illness, Joann still managed to tolerate these disruptions for the sake of our relationship. Despite our efforts to hold our relationship together, the honeymoon phase could only last so long. As the fire between us started to dwindle I began searching for a way out.

JoAnn was never the issue. Like my mother, I had a propensity to push caring and supportive people out of my life. Only I was too much of a coward to admit it to anybody, including myself. It seemed the only sensible solution to my predicament was to give her a good enough reason to bail out. To kick things off, I started taking notice of other girls and before long she began to suspect me of cheating. My irresponsible behavior was sure to result in my freedom to leave town for good. When I finally did go astray, it only happened once and with some random girl from an internet chat room. How very cliché! Oddly enough, I just couldn't bring myself to admit this indiscretion to JoAnn.

Whenever she would bring my loyalty into question, part of me was always on the verge of coming clean. In some strange way I could sense she already knew. Yet the more she persisted, the more I resisted. At one point it felt as if JoAnn and my mom were practically the same person, especially since both were always accusing me of one thing or another. Did I really leave my mother behind only to trade up for a younger version? Fearing that was the case, I decided to cut all ties with JoAnn and return to the life of an ineligible bachelor.

Ernest Hemingway wrote, "There is no hunting like the hunting of man, and those who have hunted armed men long enough and liked it, never care for anything else thereafter." My romances were typically short-lived because I much preferred the thrill associated with the whole catch and release game. After years of charming my way into women's beds, the idea of settling down never really felt like a viable option. Then again, I hadn't planned on ever falling in love. By the way, if you want to make God laugh, tell him your plans.

The breakup with JoAnn lifted a tremendous weight off my shoulders but this sense of relief was to be fleeting. I soon discovered that she was dating a mutual acquaintance. Suddenly, the urge to win her heart had never been stronger. The freedom I had once longed for somehow paled in comparison to the thought of losing her to someone else.

My strategy for winning her back was simple - just one-up the other guy. As any good tactician will tell you, inside information is vital to victory. All I had to do was pretend to care about the success of her new relationship and she would eventually trust me enough to divulge the chinks in their armor. This information would provide me with enough ammunition to take out the competition.

Once the opportunity presented itself, I made my way over to her job to begin work on the master plan. Unfortunately, I found it difficult to maintain my composure that day and even had an emotional breakdown on the drive over. A part of me felt extremely conflicted with what I was about to do. Still, I finally managed to pull myself together and entered the building. JoAnn signaled me over to a back office. Once in private, I scrapped my plan and just went with begging her to come back to me. After listening to my whole heartbroken spiel, she told me she would need some time to think it over.

I couldn't wait and take the risk of the other guy simply waltzing out the door with my prize. To kick the whole thing up a notch, I decided to sweeten the pot with a marriage proposal. That was apparently all it took to push her over the edge and clinch the win. It still baffles me to think how I honestly believed my intentions were sincere. But no sooner had the smoke cleared from the battlefield when it became apparent that my heart just wasn't into it. Had my ego not been behind the wheel from the outset, the entire complicated mess could have been avoided. Sadly, she put all her faith in my promise. The spell I was under finally broke the moment she started planning our wedding. My abrupt lack of interest was so obvious that it absolutely devastated her. The only thing left to give her was the truth.

As it happened, losing everything gave me the opportunity to put all my indiscretions on the table at once. Confessing my transgressions finally relieved me of the burden that had weighed on me for so long. Despite my repeated past denials, JoAnn admitted sensing the truth all along. We always did have a strange sort of unspoken communication between us that far surpassed simply finishing one another's sentences.

Coincidentally, this long overdue talk made us both realize how much we truly missed each other. Believe it or not, moving in together again didn't seem all that unrealistic. Despite our failure as lovers, we more than excelled in friendship. Being given a second chance imbued me with a sense of vigor I had never known before. This invigoration gave rise to a burning desire to pursue my childhood dream of becoming an actor. In hindsight, acting was merely the excuse to justify getting out of "Dodge" for good. Besides, continued entanglement with my mother's illness would only lessen the odds of achieving success in any field. Leaving San Antonio wasn't just a dream; it was an absolute necessity.

Although I became somewhat fanatical about developing a scheme to move to California, JoAnn felt the need to commit several more years to working and attending school in San Antonio. Therefore, this transition to Los Angeles was to become the solo act that would inevitably separate the two of us one last time. Despite the risk of never seeing me again, she remained true to her personal goal of becoming a teacher. I learned the meaning of commitment from that devotion.

On the evening before I left town the weather suddenly turned fierce with heavy winds. The energy in the atmosphere mirrored the turmoil and excitement welling up inside me as I began to load my possessions into the car. That night JoAnn and I slept beside each other for the last time in the apartment we once called home. The next morning she left for work and I headed over to my mom's house to respectfully bid her adieu. Sadly, she lambasted me for abandoning her just as my father had done. That accusation merely reinforced my resolve to never look back as I drove from town.

A sign stands just outside the city limits that reads: "Now Leaving San Antonio." I interpreted it as a symbol marking the initial point of my own reconstruction. The unknown horizon ahead would undoubtedly initiate me into a life of self-reliance. Dependency was a way of life growing up. Even by age twenty-one I had never known what it was to live on my own. Buck-passing had also become a tool to evade personal responsibility. And why not? I had learned from the master herself - Mom.

Though I depended heavily on her growing up, she had become far more reliant on me over the years. Moving in with JoAnn was the first step toward breaking that unhealthy cycle of interdependency. Little did I know my issues would accompany me everywhere. Regardless, the road ahead was my only chance at salvation. During the westward drive, buckets of tears streamed down my face for at least the first fifty miles. Thankfully, the well ran dry after the hundred-mile marker.

In the days preceding my departure I bought a used video camera to keep a video diary of my westbound journey. The footage includes a few interviews with random strangers plus a personal commentary on the various landscapes along the way. One such interview was conducted during a pit stop in Sedona, Arizona. I encountered a woman tending a curio shop who had no objections to appearing on camera.

After exchanging formal introductions, I presented her with a query: "What is your personal philosophy for staying afloat in life?" She uttered the following three words: "Love is everything!" Then, as if to add emphasis, she paused for a moment and added, "Plus a good man to shop with and chocolate." I told her that men and shopping didn't necessarily go hand in hand, but despite my personal assessment, she vowed to remain hopeful. Realizing the pessimism behind my comment, I replied, "We live in a world of infinite possibilities." To which she remarked, "Amen brother!"

The word *hope* is synonymous with words such as *aspiration, desire* and even *expectation*. A mentor once told me that releasing expectation cleanses the doors of perception which then allows the infinite to shine through. As with my own journey to Los Angeles, I made it a point to stop caring about the outcome. Even so, not knowing wasn't an excuse for abstaining from action. I intended on moving to Hollywood no matter the consequences. Still, my friends could only point out the potential pitfalls, despite never attempting such a major life change themselves. From a historical standpoint, no one has ever lived my life before. If I was to be the first, why not make it extraordinary?

Somewhere around the Arizona/California border I noticed a car in the rearview mirror that had been trailing behind me for quite some distance. After I slowed down dramatically, the suspicious vehicle pulled up beside me to reveal three gorgeous ladies who drew my attention by making sexually suggestive gestures with a banana. I couldn't resist pulling out my camera to capture a still of this random meeting between strangers along the desert highway.

Among the possessions in my car was a teddy bear that had been given to me years ago by an old friend. I had it riding shotgun from the very beginning of the trip. Oddly enough, just having it there produced a soothing effect amid the unfamiliar terrain. One of the girls noticed that it was all buckled in for safety and just went nuts over it. What kind of gentleman would I have been not to give it to her?

All the while they had been cruising on the passenger side of my car. So I motioned for them to pull over to the driver's side. After making my intentions clear through various hand gestures, we pulled our cars close to one another. We then proceeded to exchange the cuddly creature at speeds in excess of seventy miles per hour. So much for putting safety first. Fortunately, we managed the transfer without a hitch.

Afterwards, we pulled off to the side of the road to briefly get to know one another. As it happened, they too were on an epic journey. Since nightfall was slowly creeping toward us, we decided to move our meeting off the road and over to the nearest city. The first place we came upon was Alice Cooper's restaurant in downtown Phoenix, Arizona. After ordering a few drinks we just sat around a table and swapped stories. I started out by telling them about my quest to become a Hollywood actor. That's when one of them pointed out that we had something in common.

These girls were all childhood friends from Boston. When one of them told the others about her aspiration to drive to L.A. and become an actress, they all decided to tag along for one last road trip together. Once the journey from Massachusetts to California was completed, her friends would hop a flight back home to Bean Town. It was awe-inspiring to think about how this journey had already aligned me with a total stranger, one enraptured by a shared ambition. In any case, as it grew late we all decided to part ways. They remained in town to rest up for the night while I continued to soldier on to California.

Getting lost on this excursion to California would have been nearly impossible since I only had to follow one highway - I10 West. It runs straight through the heart of San Antonio and ends right by the Pacific Ocean in Los Angeles. Unfortunately, the countryside along the way is about a scenic as a strip mall parking lot. But on the plus side, the stars above shine brighter than a Vegas casino due to the lack of ambient lighting.

One might say that before this adventure, I too was living in a kind of barren wasteland. Owing to my mom's condition, countless demands were made on me so I rarely thought to do anything on my own initiative. Initially, it was easy to justify this empty existence to myself and others, but another part of me simply refused to accept these conditions. This emotional split often left me feeling completely isolated from the rest of the herd. What better place for a lonesome drifter to wander than on the open road.

Some heroes have a trusty steed to carry them toward adventure. In my case, that stallion turned out to be a 1995 Mustang. She's obviously more horsepower than horse which is probably why I never thought to give her a name. Nonetheless, we have had a long-standing relationship that has spanned several states and even an ocean.

After graduating high school I got a job working at a car wash. It was there that I first came across the Mustang body style that had recently replaced the boxier model. A few years later I managed to save up enough money to buy one from a used car lot. It was teal green with a V6 engine, not exactly what I had in mind, but the price convinced me otherwise. The salesperson said it only had one previous owner, supposedly a little, old lady who drove it to market and back. I took him at his word which was probably as good as any politician's.

We've now been together for nearly two decades and even though newer versions keep rolling out, none possess her allure. Much like me, she has also undergone several transformations. Years of meager wages meant the upgrades didn't happen overnight, but in a way, bleeding and sweating over this car solidified my relationship with it. Over time, that horrendous, teal green exterior was converted to silver and the standard 3.8-liter engine was made to run even more efficiently with a few minor modifications. In all these years I've not seen sufficient reason to trade up. She presently remains my trusty steed.

Prior to my journey westward I had been content with the idea of maintaining a lifelong career with USAA. For years they maintained the reputation as one of the few companies in town that could extend a lifetime of employment to all of their personnel. However, in order to ride out the weak economy, they were forced to lay off employees for the first time in their eighty-year history. Many seasoned individuals suddenly found themselves out of a job with nothing more than a severance package to show for their years of devoted service. I was almost certain that I would be one of the many sent to the chopping block, but surprisingly that wasn't to be the case. Still, the experience served as a kind of wakeup call that would help to initiate me onto a path toward my destiny. Were I to stay, the fate of my employment would always be in the hands of others.

Everything I needed to kick start my new life was already in place. I had few restrictions on internet usage, making research for lodging and employment opportunities significantly easier. I managed to reserve a room with weekly rates over in Long Beach, California, that would serve as my home base while seeking a more permanent living situation. I then began to stockpile money for a preliminary trip to Los Angeles while also setting aside a separate reserve with sufficient funds to sustain me for at least three months.

A few weeks later I flew out to L.A. over a holiday weekend to begin the housing search. When I arrived at the prearranged accommodations in Long Beach, my landlord offered me the choice of either a futon or recliner chair to sleep on. To make his own rent he was subletting every available space to anyone who could afford to pay him fifty dollars a week. He even sweetened the deal by throwing in unlimited internet usage. The level of sacrifice I was willing to make at the time still astounds me, but there I was, a kid who rarely strayed far from home was now sleeping on a futon in some stranger's living room in Long Beach, California. It seems a firm conviction can help anyone overcome just about anything.

The following morning I had compiled a list of potential dwelling prospects moments before the car rental agency picked me up. When I disclosed the purpose of my visit to the gentleman behind the counter, he offered me a Tomas Guide to use for directions. Think GPS without the aid of satellite technology. By day three I had already visited at least ten different places. In some cases I was astounded by what some considered suitable living arrangements. It seemed as though anyone with a spare corner to rent was doing so. Then there were the reasonably priced rooms featuring all the amenities I could ever want or need but those usually got snatched up within minutes of hitting the presses.

By day four the strain from my relentless searching finally took its toll. That morning I parked my rental by a metered spot in front of the Writer's Guild of America building on the corner of Hollywood Way and Magnolia Blvd. The space was conveniently located by a pay phone that I used to inquire about another room for rent. As it had become customary, the voice on the other line said, "Sorry, it's just been rented." Afterwards, I walked over to my car, leaned up against the passenger side door, and just started crying out loud.

I can remember asking myself, "What am I doing here?" The thought of resigning myself to a complacent life in Texas occurred to me but flew in the face of all the effort it took for me to get this far. That is when I knew I had to pull it together. Moving across the country was a courageous feat to attempt on my own and much like overcoming the fear of roller coasters, I would have to possess the correct attitude to achieve success. Considering the stakes, why not give myself an opportunity to get the hang of things before throwing in the towel. After all, you've got to crawl before you can run. In my case, I had to cry before I could rejoice.

Later that day I visited a prospect in a part of town called North Hollywood. The room for rent was reasonably priced and the house manager said it was only blocks from the 101, whatever that was. In any case, there was still one more place to check off the list, so I continued on my way and that's when it hit me, literally! Just as I was making a U-turn, a truck traveling in the opposite direction ran a red light and T-boned my rental - on the driver's side! The initial shock must have blocked out the pain because it certainly crept up on me several hours later. Luckily, I walked away with only a few minor scratches from the window that shattered on the side of my face.

Thanks to the optional insurance, the rental company upgraded me to a larger vehicle at no additional cost. Strangely enough, I usually opt out of the additional protection but as fortune would have it, this wasn't one of those times. Interestingly, the tow truck that hauled away the wreckage had a placard that read, "We meet our clients by accident." It's a clever motto that communicates a certain amount of truth, because in my experience nothing happens by accident.

Later that day I visited the last prospect on the list, but when it turned out to be a total shack, the North Hollywood house suddenly seemed like my ideal nesting place. After all, it was situated in a quiet neighborhood ending in a cul-de-sac just blocks from the 101 which I later discovered was adjacent to Hollywood! Furthermore, after visiting that particular residence a random accident literally stopped my car dead in its tracks. As far as I was concerned, there was no need to continue tempting fate. After securing the lease with a deposit, I flew back to Texas to issue my two-week notice. Mission accomplished!

PART III

⌘

Initiation

CHAPTER I:

First Stop: Hell

The trek from Texas to Los Angeles took a total of five days. Years later I would make that same trip, many times, in just under twenty-four hours. The maiden voyage took quite a while longer owing to my many pit stops along the way. After being stuck behind the wheel for several days, across miles of nothingness, it was a huge relief to finally arrive at my new home in North Hollywood. The room I chose to rent was situated in a five-bedroom house that was home to an array of interesting characters, including a few with no real sense of direction. Even though I felt like a fish out of water, my roommates made an effort to dispel my fears by sharing their knowledge of the world with me.

One of my roomies was a kid from Jersey with a feverish ambition to take Hollywood by storm. His father back on the east coast had a few friends in high places out west. Jersey, as I'll call him, wasn't in town for more than a month before he scored himself an agent. Meanwhile, I couldn't land an agent even if an air strip were painted down the center of my back. I once spotted Jessica Simpson wearing a T-shirt that summed it up perfectly. It read, "Talentless But Connected."

Jersey once took a moment to size me up. He started out by saying that I wasn't a bad looking kid. All I lacked was confidence. I confided that auditioning was never my strong suit. That is when he outlined a simple solution to my problem. He said, "You have to walk into every audition with the words *Fuck You* printed across your forehead!" In his mind, thinking like a bad ass wasn't enough. The attitude had to exude from every pore of my body.

Although swearing wasn't my forte, I could readily see where Jersey was coming from. One of the origins for the work *Fuck* suggests it to be an acronym meaning Fornication Under Consent of the King. Supposedly, if a couple wanted to have a child back in the day they would first need permission from the king, unless they were royals. If their request was approved, the king would issue a placard to them engraved with the letters F.U.C.K. However, in modern society, *fuck* is used to express a complete lack of consent or approval toward an idea or suggestion.

Jersey was essentially trying to make the same point. I had to walk into every audition believing that the casting agent's approval meant absolutely nothing to me. Once the need for acceptance was discarded, my actual performance could prevail. Otherwise, I could easily default into the self-defeating mental game of ricocheting between what I feel is right and what they might expect. After taking his advice to heart, it soon became apparent that he was onto something. Some of my best auditions occurred when I cared little about the outcome and relinquished all expectations. The only thing that mattered was the present moment.

It's not as if I started booking every gig thereafter, but the experience taught me that good choices are derived out of earlier poor ones. I have yet to read a bio on anyone who got it all right straight out of the gate. Often, Hollywood newcomers can appear to achieve success practically overnight, but the reality is that their success was the result of years of preparation. As one Latin phrase put it, *Amat victoria curum* - victory loves preparation.

All of those years suffered under the duress of a mentally ill parent weren't in vain. They essentially prepped me for the journey out west as well as the many others that followed. Thanks to my apprenticeship with Willy, carpentry became a skill that would serve me later in life. First off, I made a deal with the owner of the NoHo house. If she would give me a hefty discount on rent, I would maintain and develop her house. My duties would include numerous repairs to the property, including plumbing, tiling and painting; in short, a total remodel.

My mom was a fan of many biblical proverbs. The one she quoted most to me was, "Give a man a fish and you feed him for a day. Teach a man to fish you feed him for a lifetime." This may explain why she never stood in the way of the opportunities that afforded me the chance to learn a craft. Even if I had to dismantle an entire wall just to learn how to put it back together again, she was game.

However, when it came to learning to play the piano, I flat out refused. She made several attempts to explain how playing the piano could open doors for me in the future. Although I could see the truth behind her reasoning, it just made more sense to use dissent as a tactical form of vengeance. This shortsighted strategy was intended to inflict guilt on her for all the strict discipline imposed upon me. In the end, I wasn't rewarded with any such retribution. Attempting to inflict pain on her resulted in creating suffering for myself. An unfortunate yet poignant example of equal and opposite reaction, wouldn't you say?

Los Angeles isn't a city for the faint hearted, so to keep pace with the daily grind one should have a hustler's mentality. This was according my other roommate from Boston who could be described as half lady, half tramp and all business. When she was a kid, her father provided for the family by pimping. The philosophy he passed over to her early on was, "Everyone pays their way through life with ass, cash or grass, and nobody eats for free." Despite the crude phrasing, I could see how it applied.

The owner of that NoHo house lived in Sacramento, California, but visited often to keep apprised of my progress with her remodeling projects. She also took a personal interest in me that was less than professional. She even went as far as to invite me to her home for Christmas. Dare I mention she was a happily married woman at the time? Marital bliss was what she reserved for her husband but an insatiable lusting for younger flesh was what she had in mind with me.

When I arrived in Sacramento that Christmas, her husband was away on business and wasn't slated to return for a week. By then I would be safely back in L.A. As my gracious hostess, she reserved a spare room for me in her home. Following a spirited evening of gift exchanging with her friends and family members, I retired to bed. Suddenly, in the dead of night, when not a creature was stirring, my bedroom door slowly swung open. I could readily tell that the shadowy silhouette entering the room was that of my landlady. Not knowing what to expect,

I pretended to be sound asleep. Perhaps seeing through my ruse, she leaned over the bed and softly whispered in my ear, "I'll be in my room alone if you care to join me." Just before making her exit, she opened my hand and placed a condom in it. Subtle.

While laying there pondering the absurdity of the sordid situation, my instincts commanded that I stay put and just sleep the whole thing under the rug. An elephant would undoubtedly be in the room over breakfast the next morning. But as we chatted over coffee, one would never know anything out of the ordinary had transpired the night before. She was as cool as a cucumber, so after thanking my host for the interesting holiday weekend, I headed back to L.A. Nevertheless, my lack of sexual cooperation would soon come back to haunt me. Suddenly, our bartering arrangement was off the table, leaving me little choice but to pay my way with cash. It was a small price to pay for keeping my honor intact, even if only for a little while.

In my experience, few things I ever gained through minimal effort ever held much value. It was only when I shed actual blood, sweat and tears that my self-worth was discovered. After all, value isn't what something is worth to the world, it's what it's worth to you. Many have often thought me to be crazy for embracing my dreams, but in the end, finding true happiness was the result of following my heart, not my brain. Learning how to take risks was the business of my next mentor.

Darius was an executive with Universal Studios, City Walk (prior to NBC's takeover) and an avid mentor of mine. His open door policy included all employees, regardless of rank. This kept the intimidation factor out of the equation. It was common for me to meet with Darius on a regular basis. During his administration, I was managing two restaurants, often simultaneously. One day Darius took me for a short stroll through City Walk. He then began to inform me of the changes being enacted by the marketing department at Universal Studios. Before 9/11, the majority of the theme park's revenue came from Europeans and Asians. Suddenly, the flow of foreign visitors had been stemmed by the events of September 11th.

To offset these losses, Universal turned its sights on the locals who seldom visited the park. Congruently, while growing up in San Antonio, I probably visited the Alamo all of once back in grade school. Had it not been for that school field trip, I might have never toured it at all. This tendency is common to countless others whose cities harbor numerous tourist attractions. Still, City Walk tirelessly promoted irresistible bargains and discounts throughout the greater Los Angeles area, essentially blanketing the city with mass marketing tools targeting locals. The strategy worked like a charm and was particularly effective among the lower income crowd, thus morphing the well-to-do foreign demographic into the everyday bargain shopper.

As always, the only matter of interest for the shareholders was the bottom line. Failing to generate revenue from new sources would, in due time, result in fewer available work hours and consequent layoffs. The same revenue was still out there, it just needed to be tapped from a different source. Darius explained that the big wig executives had invested a substantial amount of money in market research to reveal the local's spending habits.

The executives learned it was paramount that this new demographic be made to feel extra special. Darius summarized Universal's approach in three words, "Perception is reality." This brief but brilliant locution instantly grabbed me, unleashing a giant burst of *ah hah*! He went on to explain that making people feel important supersedes their actual importance. This fostering of "specialness" among the patrons would surely yield the influx of new revenue they were after.

This new demographic may have lacked sophistication but they possessed something substantially greater - spending power and an appetite for distraction. The term spending power is an oxymoron of sorts. It's typically those who refrain from frivolous spending who tend to harbor more power. Still, bestowing a sense of importance upon the masses would, they reasoned, flatter their egos and render them highly suggestible.

Hordes of new park attendees were given the red carpet treatment. It has been said that the rich could give away all their money to the poor and within a short time they would have it all back. If you've ever wondered why the rich get richer and the poor get poorer, study the tactics used by the major corporations. Advertising in particular is geared to gain control over people's spending habits. Creating need where there was none is at the root of big business success.

Darius' insights triggered a torrent of self-inquiries. What habits or characteristics directly impeded my own happiness, health, and wealth? Moreover, how could I root out these self-limiting characteristics? During my time as a restaurant manager for City Walk I was on the edge of financial instability. Despite an already intense work schedule, incessant demands from upper management continued to pile up around me. Reality set in when I realized the busboys netted more income than their supervisor - me.

Only this time, instead of looking for someone to blame, I began to recognize the opportunity within every failure. In some circles it's believed that everything emanates from ourselves, including what we fear, lack, hate, and love. All of those things are manifested from within and not from some outside source. This explains why Gandhi preached that we must become the change we wish to see in the world. Change the world within and the outside world will change accordingly.

In leadership, fault rests on the head of the one in command. Heavy indeed is the head that dons the managerial crown. I found myself living paycheck to paycheck. My life had become a vicious cycle of lack and frustration. To add further insult to injury, all of my triumphs at work were exploited for less than ten dollars an hour. How could this have happened?

For starters, I moved to L.A. in pursuit of the whole acting thing. In hindsight, acting was merely my excuse to escape an unstable mother. The dread associated with squandering my best years in a toxic family relationship inspired me to take drastic action. But my journey to Los Angeles would ultimately reveal the genuine blessings hidden within those very same abandoned relationships.

Before leaving San Antonio I had managed to set aside enough funds to sustain me for roughly three months. I would have to acquire a job, and fast. The first gig I landed in the City of Angels was working for Universal Studios, City Walk. I was hired as a host for Gladstone's restaurant, locally noted for serving the best clam chowder in town. After providing six months of exceptional hosting to the fine people of Los Angeles, I was offered a position as a shift manager. I was initially confused as to why upper management wanted to recruit me, of all people, for the position. It seemed a bit suspicious, especially since I thought promotions entailed a series of steps through the pecking order.

Originally, I was only interested in a server position, but during my evaluation, management assured me that I belonged on their team. Furthermore, the perks would supposedly offset the pay cut. But hard work isn't always remunerated with appropriate compensation. Little did I know that my enhanced responsibilities would only yield a fifty cent pay increase per year. Management also failed to mention the countless hours of unpaid overtime they expected to get out of me.

So my career in restaurant management began with a handshake and an ardent, "Congrats." At first, the position had loads of appeal. The Hollywood acting circuit may have thought little of me, but at City Walk I was a god among men. Management was like a key to the city that allowed me to barter on just about anything in the park. Membership certainly had its privileges, but even fringe benefits lose their luster in the face of tireless, grudging work.

Finally recognizing my predicament, I scheduled a meeting to discuss stepping down from management to become a server as I had originally planned. But as usual, higher management maintained their ground by explaining that a downgrade of my status might seem like favoritism to some of the other servers. Yeah, their reasoning didn't make much sense to me either. As I had discovered, management recruits were hard to come by, so when a sucker got caught in their net they were there to stay.

My world had become reduced to a six-day a week work routine. Even my social network was whittled down to only a few co-workers. I even spent my one day off just loitering around Universal Studios. Management didn't pay enough to make venturing beyond the park alluring. At least I never had to grapple with L.A. traffic. When overcome by weariness I would often ask myself, "Wasn't it venturing out into the unknown that got me in this mess to begin with?"

Over the following three years I worked with disdain because upper management controlled every aspect of my career. They were extremely efficient at keeping employees under the minimum number of hours required for receiving medical benefits. I essentially became a living, barely breathing cliché;

overworked and underpaid. After spending my second New Year's Eve in a row stuck behind a desk at work, I was compelled to reevaluate my situation. I can remember gazing at the crowds of locals and vacationers outside. They appeared so happy and carefree. All the while, I was dying on the inside. Another year had vanished before my eyes and what did I have to show for it? I sat on a bench outside the restaurant and asked myself, "What am I still doing here?"

Beliefs can make powerful allies or troublesome adversaries. Failing to update or rethink outdated ideas may transform a formerly beneficial belief into an obstacle. When I began to formulate plans for travel or possibly even moving to a new city, the impulse was invariably crushed by mounting debts. Then one day it occurred me; debt can be paid down from anywhere in the world. So what is keeping me here? Work opportunities must surely exist everywhere. I'd much rather thrive in my own paradise than just get by in hell. If moving was the immediate goal, all I needed to do was pack my debt and go!

This simple yet profound realization lit me up like Christmas. Coincidentally, upper management scheduled an assessment meeting that very week to discuss my performance. During the meeting they indicated that failing to increase productivity would lead to my permanent dismissal. I took that threat as my resounding call to action. Without a hint of hesitation I said, "I'll save you the trouble. I'm officially giving you my two-week notice!" In that moment the road ahead appeared a little uncertain, but at least I was finally on my own path.

Over the next two weeks I began piecing together the elements of a celebratory house party. One of the privileges granted to managers was unlimited access to alcohol. What better time to take full advantage of that previously unused perk? I began stockpiling booze in the fridge back home, instructing my roommates to lay off of it until the grand finale. Abstinence was no easy task for a bunch of out of work actors, but they cooperated just the same.

During my final shift at City Walk I proceeded to get hammered, making the entire evening seem surreal. Every customer complaint was countered with generous leniency. I became the king of complimentary this and that. Not the norm for a once hard-nosed manager. Also, in an effort to get everyone out by closing time, I had the servers crank the music to an almost deafening level. Besides, higher management encouraged excessive volume levels in the dining area because it supposedly fostered a sense of anxiety in the room that would result in additional consumption. That may or may not have been true, but no one stuffs themselves at a rock concert.

When the shift was finally over, I closed up shop and headed off to my stellar house party already in progress. Filling a fridge with beer and wine over a two-week stretch can really add up. It also goes without saying that my house guests were more than happy to put it all away. During those final two weeks I made no effort to plan for what might lie ahead. Quitting that stressful job was only part of the overall goal. I primarily wanted to extend first-rate service to all of my patrons before departing "the Walk" forever. I truly believed that my courageous act would soon yield its reward, so why not show a little class on the way out?

I've heard work defined as, "Doing something when you'd rather be doing something else." Lately, work had overshadowed the outlets I often enjoyed the most. However, immersing myself in a hobby always generated a sense of internal equilibrium. So perhaps morphing a hobby into a full-time career would promote that sense of well-being I so craved. Even the thought of taking a vacation would be abhorrent because it would take me from my favorite pastime – my work.

Pursuing an acting career in Hollywood was a dream of mine that mostly occurred when I slept. But by age 26 I had finally mustered the courage to leave the familiarity of Texas in an attempt to realize that dream. The only problem was that agents weren't exactly breaking down my front door. Unemployed and on the prowl for work, I championed the phrase, "Follow your bliss." But what profession would I love as a source of income? I was already bartering handyman work for a reduction in rent. Why not expand that opportunity into the private sector and hone my skills? After placing an ad online as a "Handyman for Hire," I began to find myself knee-deep in work.

When it comes to craftsmanship, the hours just fly by. The level of concentration every project requires keeps my focus off the clock and on point. When multiple work requests poured in there never seemed to be enough hours in the day. Some days I was a landscaper while others a painter or carpenter. More importantly, a part of me was now immortalized in every client's home. Following my bliss led me out of a dead-end job and into a rewarding pastime that even paid well. Now the idea of returning to a nine-to-five job seems utterly ridiculous, and although I don't believe handyman work was ever my ultimate calling, it did provide an outlet for my creative nature to flourish until the next thing came along. Just because a raft carries one to a distant shore doesn't mean it has to be taken on the next leg of the journey.

Turning a blind eye to happiness would certainly have catapulted me to the Dark Side. Fortunately, learning to recognize the enlightening aspects of adversity turned me back toward the light. The crucial step toward initiating my personal reconstruction involved following my bliss, where ever it might lead. In medieval mythology, heroes were often portrayed as ordinary folk who somehow managed to summon the courage to sacrifice themselves for a society, cause or idea. Sacrificing comfort and convenience for the sake of my bliss is what ultimately awakened my heart to the call of adventure and ignited my desire to travel toward an unknown horizon. Perhaps Hawaii would not be just another pipe dream.

Chapter II:

The Webs We Weave

In his lectures, Joseph Campbell often quoted verses from a letter written by Chief Seattle, the namesake of the largest city in the state of Washington. Among those many verses, the following struck a chord with me, "This we know: the earth does not belong to man, man belongs to the earth. All things are connected like the blood that unites us all. Man did not weave the web of life; he is merely a strand in it. Whatever he does to the web, he does to himself."

I was granted the opportunity to experience this "web of life" phenomenon in grand fashion. My lesson involved a mentor who has since moved on. Her name was Betsy Olsen and she lived to be 94. We were introduced through a handyman client of mine. Just before our introduction, my client briefed me on some of her peculiarities. A "miserable old bitch" was one of his nicer descriptors for her. But my need for the income greatly outweighed her potentially disagreeable temperament.

The day we were to meet, my client had me stand at her doorway while he rang the bell. After listening to the sound of multiple locks being undone on the other side, the door slowly opened. A frail, white-haired woman appeared in the doorway. She smiled at me as though she recognized me from somewhere. After exchanging initial pleasantries, Betsy and I shook hands. Something in her handshake seemed vaguely familiar to me.

After I had completed a series of repairs around her house, Betsy invited me over for coffee, dessert and a bit of friendly conversation. Her gesture seemed fitting as it is not uncommon for an elderly person to enjoy new company, or any company, since they so often live alone. We steadily became better acquainted following a series of visits. While seated at her kitchen table, both of us would exchange stories over pie and black coffee.

Black coffee was never my thing, but she challenged me to try it for a week sans the sugar and cream. She assured me that once I went black, I wouldn't go back. Her belief stemmed from a Turkish proverb: "Coffee should be black as hell, strong as death and sweet as love." Betsy enjoyed all her beverages in their natural state. As she saw it, the essence of any drink would be ruined once sullied by chasers or sweeteners. She enjoyed getting to know her food in a somewhat personal way. In a sense, she allowed the food to dictate its needs to her rather than the other way around. She had acquired this unique outlook from her late spouse, Ollie.

Ollie was once a member of the U.S. Army Band. After completing his standard four-year contract, he went on to become a traveling musician and composer. He even made several arrangements for Warner Brothers Studios. After sharing a few morsels about her lost beloved, Betsy then presented me with a gift. It was a booklet titled, "Soldier's Guide to the Japanese Army." It outlined intimate details, recovered by U.S. intelligence, regarding all aspects of the Japanese military machine.

It was published in 1944, so the paper naturally exhibited signs of aging. Even the cover was partially bound with Scotch tape. The first page begins with the statement, "SHARE THIS COPY!" followed by: "Although there are not enough copies to provide for every man, it is possible for every soldier to read the Guide. PLEASE PASS THIS COPY AROUND." I was amused that fate would place this significant component of U.S. history directly into my care. I thought it to be a generous gesture on her behalf and I was very honored to receive it. Even so, the devil seated over my left shoulder was already speculating as to its worth on eBay.

Eventually Betsy saw fit to divulge the story of how Ollie and she became star-crossed lovers. When she first set eyes on him, he was standing at the butcher's counter in a local grocery store and though the two exchanged glances, no words were spoken. Ollie paid for his items and walked out the door. Betsy rushed to the counter to inquire of the butcher as to the identity of that towering man. Ollie stood over six feet tall while Betsy stood in the lower five-foot range. She discovered that Ollie was a regular by whose shopping routine you could set your watch.

The butcher let her in on a little secret. As it turned out, Ollie had been the first to take notice of Betsy in the weeks prior. Fast forward to a week later and right on schedule, Ollie walks through the door to find Betsy patiently waiting at the butcher's counter. After a brief introduction by the butcher, the two immediately hit it off. Before they knew it, wedding bells were chiming. They were married in The Little Brown Church in Studio City California. Betsy continually reminded me that Ronald Reagan wed Nancy Davis in that very church.

For their first anniversary, Betsy wanted to give Ollie something bearing significant sentimental value. Since he was a devout Catholic, a Saint Christopher pendant seemed appropriate. Saint Christopher is the patron saint of travelers and as Ollie was a traveling musician, it was the ideal keepsake. Before presenting him with it, Betsy took the sterling silver St. Christopher pendant to a Catholic church and had it blessed by a priest.

She told me he wore that pendant every day up until his death. Immediately after sharing that tale with me, Betsy then opened her frail little hand and displayed that very pendant. She then insisted that I accept it for my own protection. Betsy added that since Ollie's passing, I was the only person she's ever met who reminded her of him. According to her, wearing his pendant would bring me the love and protection of both a Saint and a father - the father of the child they never had.

After accepting her gift, I began to develop an aversion to wearing jewelry. At the outset, I only wore it whenever she requested my company for the occasional visit. But somehow, just being in possession of it seemed to dispel my disinclination toward wearing it. Suddenly I found myself wearing it all the time, even while showering. When I relayed this experience to Betsy, she conveyed the idea that Ollie was compelling me to keep it on for protection. Evidently, this was also to be regarded as evidence of his approval for having me in her life. That pendent also gave me the sense that in some way Betsy wanted to protect their only child, a role in which she had apparently cast me.

After a series of miscarriages, Betsy and Ollie abandoned any hope of conceiving a child together. They did not give up the idea of becoming parents, however, and so adopted an assortment of animals. As far as they were concerned, any of God's creatures was as good as family. Betsy even kept family photos displaying ducks, chickens, dogs and other wildlife assembled throughout their home. One photo showed a cat taking a nap inside of a bird's cage. Supposedly this was the result of some sort of daily feud between their cat and cockatoo involving the hostile takeover of the cage. Whichever proved to be the dominant one of the day won the privilege of occupying the cage. Apparently the bird lost that round.

Their first adopted newborn was a puppy that had been given to Ollie in the middle of a road tour. Someone living on the street offered it to Ollie who simply couldn't turn it down, knowing it would tickle Betsy to pieces. And so the pup joined the orchestra during the last leg of their tour. Ollie couldn't envision leaving such a tender young ankle biter alone in a hotel room for hours. As a solution he kept it cuddled in the pocket of his overcoat that lay draped over his orchestra chair. Even though instruments where blaring all around, the newest band member supposedly never made a sound. During intermissions Ollie would take the pooch out of his coat pocket to feed it milk and give it the occasional pee break. Then by the end of the week the dynamic duo came home, Ollie to his beloved and the pup to his brand new mommy.

On a day much like any other, Betsy called me over for what had become a routine visit. While seated across from me she asked if I would like to have her mint condition 1985 Mustang LX that had been sitting in the garage just collecting dust. The question alone nearly made my face go numb. It almost seemed as if I was imagining her asking that which I wanted to hear. But sure enough my ears had not deceived me and I graciously accepted her offer on the spot. But again that little devil atop my shoulder began scheming of ways to turn this beautiful gesture into some much needed cash.

Because there was no need for me to own two Mustangs, I asked Betsy if my mother could take it instead. She agreed to the idea without the slightest reservation. Shortly thereafter the title was placed in my name. The reality was that I had no intention of ever shipping it off to my mother. Instead, I immediately found a buyer for it on eBay. Betsy, of course, was not wise to this and would routinely inquire how my mother was enjoying the car and I always gave her the same update, "My mom is absolutely elated with it!" In actuality, my mom was also in on the lie and would even call Betsy to express her gratitude for the sake of keeping up appearances. The money from the sale had helped my mom and me out a lot, but it was nothing in comparison to what was headed my way next.

During another one of our visits, Betsy asked if I would like to have her house after she passed. This time, I almost fell right out of my seat. The offer was too unbelievable to pass up as I had always expressed a desire to her about owning my own home. It appeared that she had been listening and scheming all along as well. Later that week Betsy drew up the paperwork with her attorney and just like that, I was in her will. Not only would I come into possession of the home but even the bank accounts that sat for years earning interest had also become part of the arrangement. Shortly after all was said and done she remarked, "Now all that's left for me to do is die."

But you know how a fish gets caught? He opens his mouth. To this day I don't exactly know what inspired me to come clean about the '85 Mustang, but before long the truth was out, and from my own mouth no less. Despite the nobility of clearing my guilty conscience, my betrayal proved too much for Betsy to handle. My error ended up costing me more than I bargained for. Betsy immediately removed me from her will and stripped away that once in a lifetime opportunity.

I refer to that leg of my journey as my million-dollar error in judgment. Why? Because the value of the bank accounts combined with that of the home I once stood to inherit amounted to roughly a million bucks. And yet most spiritual teachings profess that perceiving anything as a mistake is indeed a falsehood. Mistakes are merely opportunities awaiting our discovery. Yet back then, in the moment, the power to embrace such a notion had been greatly overshadowed by my own disappointment and disbelief.

Still, hindsight steadfastly remains 20/20. Though it appeared I had once again found myself on the losing end of an error in judgment, another life lesson was already gearing up behind the scenes - honoring friendships. Despite all of my shenanigans, life seems to insist on propelling me toward personal growth. As with most of my shots in the dark, gaining wisdom from failure tends to open doorways to redemption. But like the crafting of a precise and powerful sword, all of my weaknesses would first have to be hammered out, whether I enjoyed the process or not.

Several days would pass before Betsy or I felt up to conversing over our usual coffee and pie. She of course had to overcome her despondency about my sudden revelation and I had to stop hating myself for orchestrating such a huge foul-up. But eventually, the two of us returned to our old habits as though nothing dubious had transpired. Over the next few days Betsy conveyed to me some of the ideals that Ollie stood for and even compared them to what she had at first seen in me.

Ollie was said to be a rare and vanishing breed of human being. Betsy saw fit to extend generosity to anyone who shared his virtues. After all, that is what Ollie would have done in her stead. To paint a clearer picture of who Ollie was in life, Betsy shared the story of his death. Ollie died of an internal gangrene infection to the lower digestive tract. Gangrene usually sets in when a large mass of damaged tissue dies entirely from insufficient blood circulation to the affected area. After tissue death, infection sets in and then it's only a matter of time before death ensues. The fatal condition was inflicted upon Ollie when he was accidentally struck by a Sears truck.

Ollie was apparently crossing the street when the truck driver suddenly lost control of his vehicle while traveling down a steep and narrow roadway. It happened so quickly that Ollie had little chance of evading the oncoming vehicle. Although he survived to tell the tale, the doctor who treated him failed to recognize the full extent of his injuries. Consequently, Ollie was diagnosed with a few broken ribs and released with nothing more than medication to help cope with the pain. During the entire ordeal, Ollie was said to have maintained a calm demeanor and ever optimistic outlook. Perhaps that's why the doctor believed everything else was fine. But Betsy wasn't buying it. She felt such an impact would surely have caused much more damage.

Nevertheless, Ollie took the doctor's medical assessment at face value and was released later that day. However, weeks later Ollie found himself crumpling over with severe abdominal pain. He was rushed to the hospital with Betsy at his side. Another surgeon insisted on performing immediate surgery to develop a clearer understanding of the injuries. Of course Betsy agreed. What he discovered was a small area of rotten, digestive tract tissue that had already infected Ollie's entire digestive system. All the surgeon could do was to administer a morphine drip to make Ollie comfortable in his final moments. That day would be his last on earth.

Ollie meant the world to Betsy and no amount of money would have compensated her loss. While Betsy desperately wanted to sue both the hospital and Sears, she also recognized that Ollie wasn't one to inflict any sort of grief on anyone, even the truck driver. When he was first admitted to the hospital, Ollie discovered that the man driving the truck had a family to support. Bringing a lawsuit against Sears would surely cost the driver his job. Being the kind of man he was, Ollie insisted that the incident was nothing more than an accident. He also instructed Betsy to refrain from suing the hospital because it would undoubtedly increase treatment costs for poorer patients.

It's not as though Ollie intended to leave his beloved in dire straits. Their house had been paid in full years ago and his pensions would be more than enough to sustain her in his absence. Betsy was always impressed with Ollie's compulsion to put her needs and the needs of others above his own. In order to honor Ollie's wishes, she relented and did not follow her own impulse to sue. Betsy was the product of Irish parents and was no shrinking violet. But if Betsy were the tempestuous winds of a hurricane, Ollie would have been its eye. His influence was the only thing that could calm her intensity. In homage to his memory, Betsy would obey the final wishes of her beloved.

In the years that followed, Betsy never once entertained the idea of remarrying. Instead, she took refuge in the home they both shared and rarely got out much. She even picked up smoking as a means of coping with her loss. This outlet evolved into a three-pack-a-day habit for the next thirty years or so. Though her friends advised her to quit, she was too headstrong to heed their advice. Betsy was determined to quit, but only when she was good and ready. Then one Thanksgiving Day, she promised her Scottish terrier, Bandit, that she would quit for good. Just like that, the habit was finished.

As for the inheritance I lost, some good still came of it. Betsy loved animals dearly. For both her and Ollie their pets were the closest thing to having children. And as Betsy saw it, if God had wanted her to bear a child she wouldn't have suffered through three consecutive miscarriages. After coming to terms with Ollie's death and never even having a child together, she turned her focus toward another cause, protecting nature's wildlife. Her way of returning the love she received over the years from an array of adopted animals was to donate generously to organizations that looked out for Mother Nature's children.

Southern California is known for its annual brush fires. Betsy knew they had a devastating effect on the animal population, so she targeted most of her contributions to the Wildlife Way Station which operates strictly on donations. When she passed away at 94, her will cited this noble charity as the sole beneficiary of her entire estate. Betsy deeply appreciated the foundation's commitment to protecting injured and orphaned animals which were victims of brush fires and other natural disasters. She believed that most animals acted more humanely than most people. Considering some of my shortsighted choices in this life, I am inclined to agree with that opinion.

Betsy had a wonderful rapport with all of God's creatures. Pushy for example, was a blue jay that flew in daily to eat peanuts right out of the palm of her hand. She gave him that moniker because he always made a shrill caw while on final approach to announce his arrival. He would then perch himself on either her wrist or head. Landing on her wrist seemed to signify that Pushy had ample time for dining in. On the other hand, if he had to dine and dash, the crown of Betsy's head was the preferred landing pad. When that would happen, Betsy would raise her hand up to her head to allow Pushy access to the goods. This delightful little ritual would certainly have seemed farfetched had I not witnessed it for myself.

Another one of Betsy's wild visitors was a squirrel she named Impy. He would make his presence known by coming up to the screen door and scratching at it. That brazen, half-pint critter would then enter the house and jump onto her lap to procure his fair share of peanuts. It's as if the wildlife that augmented their welfare with Betsy's largesse also held complete trust in her. Those little moments in particular helped me realize that my error in judgment wasn't the tragedy I had originally thought. Her final act of generosity undoubtedly enriched the lives of much wildlife. What better outcome could I have asked for than that?

Besides, had I garnered such a massive inheritance all at once, who knows what would have become of me. Years of lacking adequate financial means had me obsessing about becoming rich one day. The only problem was that I lacked any experience in the field of building wealth. Instead, I had the opposite tendency of squandering whatever money came my way. Additionally, had I been granted that inheritance, the plans that life had in store for me might have never come to pass. The people I've met in the time since have provided extraordinary experiences that truly took my journey to a whole other level. Ultimately, the inheritance I lost was merely the prelude to many assorted lessons reaped from both angels and devils.

But before her departure, Betsy still had a thing or two to teach me about the art of finding true love. Her spin on the subject ultimately led me to the realization that I had been a fraud for most of my life without even knowing it. Concerning finding that one true love, she simply remarked, "When you find that person you will just know." Years later, that person would find me and what she had to teach would open up a vast realm of potentialities within me. I would only have Betsy's sage advice to cling to until then.

When Ollie married Betsy the two were practically inseparable. They didn't have everything in common, but their lives were made whole by learning and growing from one another. Ollie was always mechanically inclined and eventually taught Betsy the fundamentals of assembling and dismantling engine blocks. When I was first taken into her garage and shown the '85 Mustang that would eventually become mine, I also caught sight of an old car covered in dust. Aside from needing a good wash, it was practically untouched by time.

The car turned out to be a 1953 Ford Crestline, Sunliner Convertible, OVERDRIVE. Since describing vintage cars in detail isn't my forte, I would encourage a brief internet search on it sometime. For an old Ford, it still oozed charisma from bumper to bumper. I also noticed an engine block hoisted alongside the car. Not only could Betsy successfully swap engines, she could also rebuild them from the ground up. She then pointed out the extensive tool collection that the pair of them had amassed over thirty years. The idea that this frail, 93-year-old woman was a grease monkey at one time certainly impressed the hell out of me. But for Betsy, it was just par for the course.

She admitted that Ollie's patience is what made it all possible. Otherwise, that Irish temper would have never gotten her past the first bolt. Although they were opposites in many respects, their individual temperaments offset one another's perfectly. It had always been my nature to shy away from anyone having views that differed from my own. I was never interested in finding "the one" because the idea seemed absurd to me. To begin with, how could I possibly know if someone was the one? Unlike Betsy and Ollie, sex was the only way I knew how to express love.

In one respect I was like Betsy in that we both were set in our thinking. Everything she held to be true about the outside world was based upon obsolete and outdated perceptions. For example, she believed that if God had intended different races to mix, He would not have placed them on different continents. Statements such as this are what made me realize how I was constrained by old patterns of thinking. One fairytale in particular expresses how a kiss from a worthy prince is the only thing that can awaken a princess from her magical sleep. Only I was the prince who slept within the toad. Perhaps the kiss of a princess would one day awaken me from that dream. Only the "kiss" would be more like a slap in the face, the kind you give someone to shock them back to their senses. Sometimes that's what it takes. But my nap would last a little longer while I awaited enlightenment.

Something was clearly influencing my attitude toward sex and love. After years of soul searching, I finally tracked the beast down in the memory of that one particular foster home all those years ago. Apart from the obvious, my offender was the first person to introduce me to porn. The details of what I saw in those magazines are long gone, but the feelings that lingered teetered on the sketchy side for sure.

I always suspected that those images somehow corrupted my interpretation of love and even friendship from an early age. While the state may have removed me from that situation, the damage had already been done. Even as a boy, my every thought regarding the opposite sex was colored with a shade of perversion. Moreover, my foster brother was always appeased by my cooperation. The alternative was to be beaten up and I had already experienced enough of that in my own home. It was inevitable that I would later interpret the use of sex as the most appropriate means of currying favor, both with lovers and female friends.

No one ever suspected the foster home abuse because my foster brother made me swear to secrecy. Because the problem had not been brought to the attention of the authorities, no measures were taken to correct the flawed course of my emotional development. Unhealthy feelings and thoughts festered for years and made it impossible to develop and maintain normal personal relationships. An opportunity to temper those thoughts also came and went in elementary school.

My mother was never an active agent in the molding of my academic career. In fact, I was able to pass every grade level by mastering the art of forging her signature. Whenever a report card required parental acknowledgment, it was my hand drafted autograph that proved my mother was aware of my scholastic triumphs as well as my many failures. Then one day I received word that our fifth grade class was slated to watch a video on human reproduction. The moment the permission slips went out, mine was likely the first to get signed before it even left campus. But on the day our class was to watch this monumental video, someone dropped the ball and misplaced my permission slip.

It wasn't a matter of being caught in the act of forgery. Had that been the case, my mother would surely have been contacted immediately. The slip had simply vanished. The only option was to leave me in an empty classroom along with another kid who also lacked the appropriately signed document. Thus the opportunity to normalize my sleazy mindset had been squandered, leaving me to wonder what mysteries everyone else might be unraveling in that forbidden room. Despite all my efforts to glean details from my classmates, no one could explain much about what they had just seen. Apparently one just had to be there.

My issues were exacerbated when I stumbled upon a late night phenomenon at my friend Manuel's house. I called it the "squiggly channel." It was a channel that was intentionally distorted for all non-subscribers by the cable company. It was quite the thrill to sit anxiously in front of the TV set hoping for the occasional momentary unscrambling of a female body part. Is it any wonder why platonic relationships with girls were so hard for me to develop? Fortunately, experience would later demonstrate that even perverts can evolve. The trick is having the desire to let go of the old so that something new can come into being.

CHAPTER III:

The Upside of Down

As cycles are supposed to go, every cursed experience is followed by a blessing. The challenge is to believe in the coming of spring while riding out the chill of winter. Curses most often develop when one acts too hastily. Blessings began to appear in my life the moment I understood that nothing is inherently good or bad; only perception makes it one or the other. In one way or another, anything we do is likely to have a negative effect on someone. My only real mistakes resulted from the choices from which I never learned. The time I spent as a restaurant manager could have been for naught. But if the Universe wastes nothing, why should I?

The Universe seemingly conspires in favor of those whose heart takes the helm. Shifting how I perceived my life made all the difference. Joseph Campbell taught his students to recognize the mythological themes evident in their own lives. According to Joseph, there is but one mythology in the world. The outer world is what you get in scholarship and the inner world is your response to it. The outer world changes with time but the inner world remains constant. Where the two meet is the myth. Myth has now become the middle ground of my own existence and has helped to restore a sense of balance in my life.

Many people perceive metaphors as fact. They are called theists. Conversely, those who believe metaphors to be lies are known as atheists. Recognizing the truth behind both points of view negates the need to fully identify with either. Life can then be seen for the cyclical journey it truly is. As a youth I had been programmed to study medicine. Although that path was never taken, physiological studies continued to captivate my interest.

Consider the journey of an embryo in becoming a baby. It can be said that everyone goes through an enormous effort just to be born. The journey of a fertilized egg, dividing many times over, is analogous to an entire life experience. The series of cell divisions ultimately yield the creation of an entire unique being. The next major transformation takes place when the child dies (figuratively) by shedding its dependency and becoming a mature, responsible adult. The sequence mirrors the whole hero act - departure, fulfillment and return.

On my own journey, fear of the unknown was my constant companion. But I maintain that fear is not the opposite of courage. Courage is taking action in the face of fear. Thinking in mythological terms can help curb natural anxieties about the true nature of life. After all, in order for life to sustain itself and beget more life, it must consume life. So does death really exist? If it does, it is likely to be found in the essence of life. In my own experience, years would go by before my inner child would die to make way for the emergence of the adult. However, an opportunity to jump on the fast track to become my own master would soon fall into my lap.

Another career exploit was presented to me almost by chance. I was given the opportunity to work for an extremely successful entrepreneur. I'll call him Mr. X. The salary that accompanied the position was more than I'd ever earned before. The money was a shiny object that distracted me from the reality of the situation. Mr. X was known by all with whom he dealt as a classic "type A" personality. It wasn't long before I discovered that failure to meet his standards would never be a viable option with this guy. Regardless, I remained eager to please and even more grateful for the opportunity.

When I was first learning how to swim, my father pushed me into the pool and trusted instinct to handle the rest. Fortunately, those instincts at least knew how to stay afloat. Mr. X was no different in his training approach. Only the pool he tossed me in was more like an institutional-sized washing machine set to *Heavy Duty* with an *Extra Rinse* cycle. Mr. X demanded more from me than I ever expected of myself. In the end, his tactics helped to dispel the lack of self-confidence I had harbored for so long.

Initially, in order to meet his expectations I had to resort to lying, cheating and even stealing. These strategies were never specifically asked of me. But in order to comply with his incessant ultimatums, survival mode kicked in and displaced any moral compunction I might have held. My soul had been sold on the open market – and cheap. This form of selling out resulted in excessive drinking, smoking and the occasional pot-induced coma, diversions intended to mitigate the stress from the job I once thought myself so fortunate to acquire.

To this day, Mr. X remains one of the most formidable human beings I have ever met. As the new-hire everyone in his office felt the need to approach me with the same question: "Do you know about Mr. X?" They even phrased the question with the same inflection. Initially my experience with the man had been a pleasant one. This led me to ask, "What is it I should know?" All I would get in response was, "You'll find out!"

I started getting the sense that Mr. X might be harboring a few demons of his own. When writers develop a horror movie script they will initially obscure the image of the monster from view. This strategy inspires the audience to imagine demons that transcend the scope of any CGI or special effects. I was now living a movie script, yet my imagination couldn't conceive of the horrors that lay ahead.

The first step toward my rude awakening started with a phone call from the boss. The first thing Mr. X told me was, "You look like a nice guy." His ability to see through people could put Superman to shame. He then proceeded to share some of his philosophy surrounding his work ethic. Mr. X, an Englishman, stated, "There's a reason why most Americans bring home less than thirty-five thousand dollars a year."

He followed with, "Most people lack essential disciplines like organization and persistence. But in this world the wheel that squeaks gets the oil. So you have to kick and scream like a little baby until you get what you're after! I always expect you to stay on point. The way I operate is to push you until you say stop. And don't expect me to know when you've reached that point. You're gonna make it here and I'll be the one kicking your ass the whole way!"

My selection for this job was starting to look like some sort of cosmic accident. But in his unique way Mr. X would soon clarify, *there are no accidents.* In fact, luck plays a huge role in success. For luck is the product of preparation and opportunity. But these lessons would not be learned until I had earned my way toward them. My L.A. handyman business nailed a perfectly executed swan dive into disillusionment. A lull in the economy was mostly to blame. Homeowners (the life-blood of my business) were suddenly upside down on their mortgages and could no longer afford my services. Forced out of self-employment, I started pounding the streets for a job.

At about that same time a friend referred me to an agency that places qualified applicants in high-end, domestic positions (i.e., maids, butlers, house managers and the like). Although they saw little promise for a handyman, my information was kept on file. The number of times "having my name of file" ever got me hired - zero. Fortunately, the agent assigned to my case worked on commission and was motivated to see me placed in a position.

Every time he called me up with a potential employer in mind, he'd say, "This is the one for you, Alex. I can feel it!" Even though the first couple of prospects he lined up didn't work out, his tenacity never faltered. Overall, he landed me three interviews. One of them was at the Brentwood estate of the deceased Beatle, George Harrison. His widow, Patricia Boyd, was looking for someone handy to maintain the property.

Entering a house that was once home to a Beatle was awe-inspiring. An oil painting of George hung at one end of a corridor. I'm guessing he was roughly in his thirties when this rendering was completed. In it, he sports a shaggy beard and long hair. Fascinating as the estate was, I must digress to the actual interview. It took place in the living room. Surrounding this space stood a medley of guitars that once graced the skilled hands of a legend. His widow, Patricia, was not present for the interview. Instead, the assignment was handled by her personal assistant. After a deluge of questions, the interview was over. I felt it could have gone either way.

But alas I wasn't a match for one of the first ladies of rock n' roll. My agent thought I may have exuded too much confidence. As he saw it, they needed someone older and a bit more settled. The position was long-term, after all. Hiring someone with ambition who would jump at the next attractive opportunity would not fit this requirement. He was correct in his assumption. Working for a star (or the widow of one) is one thing; becoming a star is a unicorn of a different color. Once I had left the comforts of home behind, discovering and reaching the limits of my potential took precedence. Undoubtedly, maintaining the home of a musical legend would, in-time, lose its luster. I suspect even George would support that notion.

So, back to the front lines of unemployment I went. And little did I know that success was right around the corner. Once again, my trusty agent set me up with another interview. Calling to inform me in the usual fashion, he said, "This is the one for you, Alex. I can feel it!" This time I would be interviewing for a position as a caretaker for a Beverly Hills estate. The client was the daughter of a former business executive, now crippled by dementia. She would also be conducting the interview. The first question out of the gate was, "Are you interviewing because of your passion for private home care or do you want the job just to have a job?" My selection of the latter option was met with resounding silence.

I realized which answer potentially weighed the odds in my favor, but the honest approach seemed the only way to go. Her query brought into question my personal passion for the career, but faking genuine passion is tough, especially for an actor with dubious talent. She wasn't about to subject the care of her father's estate to someone with little interest in the position.

But before dismissing me, the potential client shared a brief history about her father. Of course, he was no George Harrison, yet he was no stranger to the dizzying heights of success. She remarked, "You wouldn't believe it to look at him, but my old man was once a powerful guy." She said that strong-arm tactics were his method of choice for getting things done and commanding respect.

Eventually, his subordinates became courtiers who would deliver only good news to their king. But the karma of his coarse behavior eventually caught up to him. Approaching retirement, he started to display early symptoms of Alzheimer's. Forced into retirement, he had nowhere to go but down. Some consider retirement to be the number one cause of death among the elderly.

His descent into oblivion took its toll on his relationships. His wife of many years eventually threw in the towel and filed for divorce. Now alone in his own little world, he developed a routine of arranging picture frames on the dining table. Like platoons of Civil War soldiers, every group was positioned in perfect rank. He would also unlace his shoes, often only re-lacing one of them. But the real challenge was escorting him out to dinner at his favorite eatery. Often, he would interact with total strangers from a nearby table, believing they were old friends. It was very apparent that I was indeed not a match for her father. And with that, my second interview was over.

Then the interview that would change everything finally arrived. True to form, my agent called me up saying, "This is the one for you, Alex." Only this time he added, "Not only do I feel it, but on paper you're practically the embodiment of what this client is looking for." When I was little my mom always told me, "Whatever you are seeking, it is also seeking you." For once, I finally felt like my agent was saying all the right things. As it turned out the client wanted a handyman for his beachfront estate in Hawaii. My skill set, once deemed of little use by the agency, suddenly catapulted me to the front of the herd.

It was as if Serendipity herself was calling me on speed dial. When I was a kid, *The Jeffersons* was one of my favorite sitcoms. George Jefferson (portrayed by the late Sherman Hemsley) was infamous for his uptight and overly ambitious attitude. He even had a strut to complement that demeanor. Then a four-part episode featured the Jeffersons vacationing in Hawaii. I watched as George's uptight attitude slowly transformed into its opposite. The island was somehow responsible for generating this inexplicable metamorphosis. From that moment I couldn't wait to make Hawaii a chapter of my life. If the islands could transform George Jefferson, perhaps they might do the same for me.

My initial interview took place in the Beverly Hills Hotel. When I arrived, the client sat with my agent at a round table near the bar where I chose to sit and wait my turn. The interview that preceded mine went on for some time. Then it was my opportunity to shine. From the moment I sat across from him it felt as though he was looking right though me. He had a long list of questions that filled several sheets of paper. Feeling discouraged after failing to succeed in either of the two previous interviews, I felt I had nothing to lose. All I wanted was to get through the interview.

After the interview I wasted no time in getting feedback from my agent. He reported, "Everything appears to be coming up roses!" Even though six other well qualified applicants were competing for the job, I still had my ace in the hole - carpentry experience. Now began the always too long waiting period. But with unwavering optimism I put off looking for other work. Before long my trusty agent called me to deliver the news, "You got the job, kid! Didn't I tell you this was the one?" Superstitiously, the third round proved to win the bout for me.

Mr. X was the answer to my prayers in more ways than one. I recall the minister saying in a church sermon from childhood, "Life doesn't always give you what you want but it never fails to send you what you need." After months without work, a huge opportunity had landed squarely on my lap. My elation was off the charts and I never once felt this could be a mistake. Were it not for the words of that minister reverberating in my mind, I would have given up on myself long ago. And sure enough, in the weeks that followed I found myself bound for Hawaii.

Prior to my departure, Mr. X sat me down and recited his rags to riches story. After dropping out of high school in England at the age of sixteen he took a job working for his father in order to familiarize himself with the restaurant business. And while he didn't start at the top, his success hinged on a series of risks that ultimately propelled him to fortune.

Soon thereafter he left England for a shot at the big time in America. He first landed in Florida. In less than a week following his arrival, a newscast warned of an approaching hurricane. The coastline where he lived was said to have incurred the largest amount of damage. For many, the news denoted impending tragedy, but for Mr. X the looming ordeal was sweet music. He immediately lashed together a business venture involving the removal of debris from properties affected by the hurricane. His quick thinking and initiative earned him a small fortune. Not a bad way to jump start an American success story.

The ability to see opportunity in a sea of chaos is an innate talent, a gift clearly bestowed upon Mr. X. After achieving some success in Florida, it was off to the Big Apple where he started out as a bouncer at a bar. Becoming a bouncer wasn't the goal as much as it was the opportunity. Always multiple steps ahead of the pack, he could see an opportunity for boundless growth.

After assembling a three-man dream team, Mr. X ventured into bar ownership. Once again, his vision had pierced through another level of achievement. While at the height of this newfound success, he set his sights on an even greater target – Las Vegas. He told his band of partners, "Let's go to Vegas and get rich!" They, along with all of his friends, thought he was losing it. How could he just jump ship and move away from everyone and everything he knew? But Mr. X saw past their doubts. After all, leaving his birthplace abroad had proven vital in achieving his financial success. As with countless fairytales, the hero never denies the impulse to travel beyond their comfort zone.

Without going into further detail, I will say that Mr. X's leaps of faith have yielded copious monetary rewards. He admitted to making many mistakes along the way. However, the key factor in winning involved learning from every misstep and doing so quickly. That small detail was one of the many differences between Mr. X and me. Even though most of my ventures didn't yield favorable outcomes, habit compelled me to repeat my errors. Much of that foolishness was the result of unconscious behavior.

The silver lining to working for Mr. X was that, unconscious or not, I would not be given any margin for error with his affairs. Some of his contemporaries compared him to a steam roller who could easily, and happily, flatten any obstacle in his path. Furthermore, he had the temper and assertive personality to back it up. Such nuggets of inside information intimidated me to say the least. At the same time his fierce intolerance for failure would prove to be an ideal remedy to cure me of some of my more senseless behaviors.

Whenever Mr. X assigned me to a task he would always say, "You'd better get it done!" The dreaded, "Or else!" was the unspoken threat. One of his most challenging tasks arose before my assignment to Hawaii. Several of his personal belongings requiring shipment to the island by freighter were stored in both Las Vegas and Beverly Hills. The challenge involved packing the items from a comprehensive list that included both locations, then transporting the load to a shipyard in Long Beach. As an extra degree of difficulty, I had to arrive at the dock before eleven the next morning, leaving me approximately sixteen hours to execute this daunting task.

The driving portion was a cake walk since I used to make an annual pilgrimage by car from Los Angeles to San Antonio just to visit my mom. Stopping only to refuel cut the driving time to under twenty-three hours. Knocking out fourteen hundred miles in under a day was the perfect preparation for my assignment which began in Nevada.

Unfortunately, the company Mr. X had contracted to load the truck didn't share his passion for punctuality. Late on the day I was scheduled to leave they still hadn't crated several of the bulkier items and their leisurely pace was starting to chip away at my drive time. But whether I liked it or not, the buck stopped with me. After all, the task wasn't about pointing fingers. Success was the only acceptable outcome, or else! As nightfall steadily crept westward, I just sat nervously on my hands until the final crate was on the truck. I was then given the option to rent a cheap hotel for the night or continue on to the next rendezvous point in California.

I opted out of resting because the laws that governed ordinary mortals didn't seem to apply to Mr. X. His reputation for inspiring foreboding in greater men than me provided ample motivation to keep me driving through the night. The last thing I needed was to risk a traffic jam in the early morning hours or even worse, oversleeping. So before entering Los Angeles I pulled into a rest stop, locked the truck down like Fort Knox, and grabbed an hour or so of sleep. That catnap was just enough to get me back into the game.

My next stop was at Mr. X's Beverly Hills home situated deep in the hills. There I was to meet with another operative and load the remaining items before making the final leg to the dock. The houses in there may be magnificent, but the streets connecting them are horrendous. Some corners and stretches are so tight that two Mini Coopers headed in opposite directions would likely knock off one another's mirrors. Yet I somehow managed to maneuver the entire course with the finesse of a Formula One driver. It's truly amazing what one can accomplish by simply ruling out failure.

Upon reaching Mr. X's house, I packed up the last of the items and headed off to the dock with an hour left on the ticker. In most cities an hour might seem like a lot of time, but the freeways of Los Angeles are unforgiving. Fortune must have been smiling upon me that day because I reached the dock with five minutes to spare. Mission accomplished!

That assignment was just a sample of the level of performance Mr. X demanded on a constant basis. My previous employers had required their own level of excellence, but none had ever applied his sort of strong arm pressure. To say he was intimidating would be a gross understatement. At the same time his uncompromising insistence on perfection was exactly what I needed to address my own character lapses. Only when the old is destroyed can the new arise from the rubble.

I've often witnessed little boys imitating their fathers. Perhaps they instinctively associate the male form with strength. But in my case it was my mom's tenacious spirit that refused to waver despite her mental illness. But another parental figure wasn't what I needed or wanted from Mr. X. Instead, he represented potentialities that I knew lay dormant within me. His coercive tactics never provided room for error. That is why I credit him alone for curing me of my propensity to make excuses.

In an effort to reinvent my personal image, I started out by implementing a wardrobe selection technique from one of my acting classes. Everything from my shoes on up was loosely based on Mr. X's attire. To get into character one must become the role in every possible sense so that the person you know yourself to be doesn't bleed into the one you're attempting to play. Whether he knew it or not, Mr. X would inevitably shift the course of a destiny riddled with problematic behavioral patterns.

Gray was an area in which Mr. X rarely dabbled. His approach involved being critical of the few things I did wrong and to ignore the greater number of tasks that were executed to perfection. Perhaps he believed positive reinforcement would extinguish my incentive to improve. One day he even said to me, "In this economy you could easily be replaced by someone who would be willing to work for half of what I pay you." After those words echoed in my head for a moment, a profound realization suddenly occurred to me; "I deserve better than this!"

Suddenly, I began reeling off the many exasperating circumstances Mr. X had put me in along the way. Something within me was finally pushing its way to the surface and for an instant I was no longer constrained by desire or fear. After all, those were the very culprits that initially got me into this mess. The fear of losing a cushy gig and the desire to pursue material gain had outweighed the instinct to follow my true passion. Truth be told, I didn't have a firm grip on the path my life should take, but a career with Mr. X definitely wasn't it.

After reigning myself back from the tirade I felt welling up within me, I was fairly sure that my permanent dismissal was imminent. But if this was going to be the end, better I should leave as a man than as a mouse. While maintaining eye contact with my employer and tormentor, I braced myself for one hell of a retort. Instead, his response took me by complete surprise. In a very genial manner he dispensed the following piece of advice, "You know Alex, it's alright to stand up for yourself."

From an early age others had always expected absolute obedience from me, so I never entertained the inclination to object. Yet this powerhouse of a human being had bestowed a grand gesture upon me which would have never come about had I continued to cower in fear. In that moment I felt that he had offered me two choices; dedicate myself to his system of personal claim on my soul or follow my bliss. Well, if I had managed to pull off several minor miracles under extreme duress with Mr. X, then perhaps that same dedication could initiate some positive momentum in my own life. What then was holding me back?

In a mythological sense, dragons are to blame. According to Joseph Campbell they symbolize the ego's hierarchy of elementary concerns involving self-interest. They guard heaps of gold and virgins in caves while making use of neither. Simply clinging to this uninspired existence inhibits their ability to act progressively. Anything that threatens to diminish their stockpile incites reactions of violence rather than compassion or understanding. I could see this in my own life, especially when the prime motivators governing me revolved around chasing skirts and working long hours to secure the money to pursue that aim.

Joseph Campbell also coined a term, "Monomyth," from James Joyce's *Finnegan's Wake*. It's a term that represents the classic sequence of actions constantly reappearing throughout many mythological narratives. For example, the first half of a journey is characterized by three distinct events: Separation/ Departure, Initiation and Return. Each event is initiated by a distinct series of trials or rites. The trial of temptation falls under a category entitled, *Woman as Temptress*.

Temptation is no stranger to a hero, especially during the initiation stage of a quest. The inclination to follow money, lust or any number of pleasures can often persuade a would-be hero to abandon or stray from his calling. In my own experience, temporary gratification never yielded much long-term value. This reoccurring theme eventually left me feeling distaste for my own nature, particularly where women were concerned. And what were these women if not a metaphor personifying my willingness to succumb to an array of temptations, especially when conflicting with an opportunity to champion a worthier cause.

Furthermore, the work that I was performing for Mr. X no longer felt like a viable resource from which to draw inspiration. One thing was abundantly clear; I had become my own dragon. But how could I slay something that was intrinsically a part of me? Buckminster Fuller was an American author, architect, inventor and futurist who suggested the following, "You never change things by fighting the existing reality. To change something, build a new model that makes the existing model obsolete."

In Fuller's view, slaying dragons didn't necessarily involve rigorous action. It did however, call for innovative thinking. Because much of my past was embroiled in fear-based thinking, that personal dragon had no trouble holding me in. That was until I stumbled across an unconventional acronym for the word *fear: false evidence appearing real*. Well, if evidence is all one needs to maintain a particular slant on reality, why not build a case to support a more favorable point of view? From then on I made it my duty to break past long-standing impediments that only served to perpetuate my stagnation.

It always seemed that Mr. X's mind was in a constant state of flux. He was a fervent guru who reveled in teaching me proven alternatives to save both time and energy, thus making my life a lot easier. I suspect he would never have taken the time to do so had I not shown early signs of promise. He constantly stressed the importance of staying on point and insisted I make punch lists to stay in alignment with my goals. He even gave me a tape recorder to dictate those objectives to myself before writing them down. This way nothing would be forgotten during the scramble to locate a pen and pad - a routine problem.

Organization, whether in thought or action, was never my strong suit, especially growing up amid the chaos of mental illness. Fortunately for me, Mr. X wasn't the least concerned with my past. Productivity was all that mattered in his world and if he were going to elicit it from me, my faulty behaviors could in no way be coddled. At this stage of my journey I was given a great opportunity to integrate effective techniques with instruction from someone who clearly had mastery over his affairs.

Friedrich Nietzsche was a German philosopher who wrote a book entitled, *Thus Spoke Zarathustra*. In it he describes the three metamorphoses of the human spirit symbolized by the camel (the social beast of burden), the lion (the lone warrior who defeats the Dragon) and the child (the new beginning). The camel's function is to receive instruction through imparted education. This knowledge can cover anything from table manners to religion. Personal experience is entirely negated. Lacking the ability to question authority, the camel allows itself to be controlled by social values. Its incentives are strongly influenced by fear and guilt, prompted by dogma.

But when the camel begins to question the origin of any principle or even desires to know its meaning, he soon finds himself alone in the wilderness, marginalized by society. That is when the second transformation takes place and the camel then becomes a lion. The lion represents a noble and vicious killer. He must be such in order to fulfill his function as a dragon slayer. And the name of that dragon is *Thou Shalt*, the name imprinted on each of its scales. Nietzsche uses the dragon to represent God. This god merely refers to the restrictions, internal and external, imposed upon all human beings from the moment of their birth.

Nietzsche implied that if someone truly wishes to have their own unique experience of life they must be reborn as a fierce warrior to slay the belief systems that halt progressive thought and action. But since the lion only knows how to destroy, another transformation must take place so that creation can begin. Hence, once the lion slays *Thou Shalt,* he is turned into a child. The child has no sense of what the world was like before the existence of camels, lions and dragons. The child simply represents a new beginning.

Cyclical progression is the overall idea behind this series of transformations. Throughout my own life, countless people instructed me on what was proper in the realm of behavior, belief, etc. Guilt and shame were used as weapons to reinforce that education. But I always had the sense that a better life was patiently awaiting me. That notion started out as a fantastic idea - suffering can't possibly last forever. Yet had it not been for suffering, the impulse to free myself from it would never have materialized.

A yearning for freedom eventually stirred me to question the beliefs that appeared responsible for most of that suffering. The hardships got easier to navigate once I learned to establish a new set of beliefs that were grounded in sound experience. It took Mr. X's fierce behavior and demeanor to help me realize the critical importance of removing old narratives from my story. Questioning both old and new ideas is an ongoing priority of mine because experience has proven that stagnation is the death of creativity.

Every pupil must inevitably become his own authority. That is precisely why I chose to dismiss myself from Mr. X's employ. How could I not take that leap? When friends urged me to consider the consequences, I couldn't help but reflect on Mr. X's personal history. He steamrolled over the fear and doubt generated by his friends and family to bring his dreams to fruition. So I concluded that the best way to honor his example was to follow it. After all, imitation is said to be the best form of flattery.

Throughout my youth several individuals imposed their wills upon me to create a compliant operative. But the moment I mustered the courage to stand up for myself, a small fissure formed in that wall of fear surrounding me. As my confidence grew, that crack got bigger and bigger until large chunks of the wall began to crumble away. In a real sense that wall never really existed. It was merely a state of mind supported by unchallenged beliefs. Had those ideologies remained intact, their irrelevance might never have been understood.

PART IV

∽⊶∾

The Return

Chapter I:

Wisdom of the Aged

I grew up around people who were well into their golden years. My mother always surrounded herself with the elderly and whenever she visited one of those human relics I invariably dreaded the invitation to tag along. Their incessant chatter wasn't likely to interest a ten-year-old boy. Because their children were nearly my mother's age I always had to be my own playmate. Regardless, her objective was to gain the sort of wisdom that only comes with age. After all, raising her own children with a mental disorder and amnesia would require some sage advice.

Subsequently, some of my most cherished advisors would also turn out to be grizzled. The grace with which they instructed often appeared to be divinely inspired. They would challenge me to incorporate daily practices from discerning minds such as Leonardo Di Vinci and Gandhi. A few of the older male patriarchs also served as father figures. In essence, much of my childhood instruction was outsourced to a wide array of characters.

One of those patriarchal figures was a dear friend of my mother's named Manuel. He was a retired postal worker and widower whose children were already grown and fully engaged with raising their own families. He also lived in the North Side Independent School District which was known for its superior educational programs. The schools on my side of town just passed students along despite their lack of any demonstrated proficiency. Because my mother wanted me to have a better education, she struck a deal with Manuel. In exchange for housing and the opportunity to attend school in a better district I would take over all the upkeep in and around Manuel's house. My list of chores included cutting the grass, mopping the floors, doing the laundry, and keeping my room and the entire house spotless.

My mom used to say, "Manuel is so tight he squeaks when he walks." Like many his age, Manuel spent much of his youth living through the Great Depression. That was likely responsible for his strict fiscal tendencies. This tightwad would introduce me to two foreign concepts, control and temperament. Before Manuel I feared that every meal might be my last. For me, quality was never as important as quantity. I grew up with an older brother who would devour everything in sight. If it wasn't nailed to the floor he would be the first to nab it, so gorging myself with whatever was available was a survival strategy. Because our food supply was anything but consistent, the behavior just stuck. I wasn't even aware of the habit until Manuel pointed it out.

Manuel had served in the Army but was discharged due to his flat feet. Although his military career was short-lived, the disciplines he acquired from the experience made a lasting impression. As far as Manuel was concerned, Army standards fit his civilian life perfectly. He even passed a few of his habits on to me. Soon I was making every bed in the house with hospital corners and scrubbing the tile grout with toothbrushes.

He also enforced strict policies when it came to food. Any food item could be taken only with permission. He assigned me a small plastic cup to limit my daily intake of juice or soda. I was also allowed to make one sandwich per day consisting of two slices of Wonder Bread, a slice of cheese, one slice of bologna and (if I really wanted to go all out) mayonnaise. Were it left up to me it would be all bologna all the time. But no one was asking for my input. These orders came crashing down like thunder and I was expected to obey. End of story. Furthermore, I could only address him as *Sir.*

I found it ironic that his kitchen was packed with food, yet it could be consumed only in precise, calculated increments. Manuel would often sit across from me to observe my eating habits. If I should begin eating too quickly he would order me to stop eating altogether. He would then set my meal aside and proceed to demonstrate a more appropriate pace with his own meal. After a few minutes of this he would hand back my meal and allow me to start over. This method was used on me until he was satisfied that my old habit of gorging had been defeated.

After completing middle school I returned home to my mother. However, this time my backbone had a bit more sturdiness to it. Manuel remained a part of my life until his death several years later. He was never the type to shower me with expensive gifts, except for once. A few years before his passing Manuel took it upon himself to buy me a basketball hoop set, complete with stand. At first glance this gesture might appear insignificant. But to me its meaning extended beyond a simple gesture of generosity. I considered it to be an unspoken message of approval from one of my toughest mentors.

In middle school sports I had to be my own cheering section. Manuel never took me to any tryouts, practices or even games for that matter. I wasn't the most astounding athlete on campus, but a little support would have been appreciated. Still, I desperately wanted to be a part of something greater, so against Manuel's wishes I earned a spot on the basketball team. Perhaps as punishment, he made it abundantly clear that I would have to manage all my own sporting events. Still, there was something about defying his wishes that gave me a sense of independence and power.

While on the team I dubbed myself the "minute man" because the coach routinely dismissed my requests for playing time by saying, "In a minute man; in a minute!" During practice, any member of the team who missed a lay-up automatically earned the entire team 10 to 20 sit-ups. Lay-ups just so happened to be my weakest shot, but because Manuel insisted I always head straight home after school, little to no time was left for practice. On the bright side, my weakness contributed greatly toward the overall fitness level of the entire team.

As time went on, Manuel's lack of support made caring about it less important. I owed my good standing with the team entirely to myself, or so I thought. Years later I would perceive Manuel's hoop set gift in an entirely new light. It wasn't just some run-of-the-mill contraption. It was the crème de la crème model and it didn't come cheap. However, it was the nature of the gift that relayed more to me than the price tag ever could. As a kid I had constantly pleaded with Manuel to get me a hoop set to practice on at home. It didn't have to be anything fancy, just the metal loop that I would even install myself. But, as usual, he flatly refused. He told me that if I wanted anything in this life it would be my sole responsibility to go out and earn it.

Previously, I never made a move without first consulting my mother. Manuel was the first to recognize this childlike tendency still lingering in me and knew that I would, one day, have to develop a sense of self-reliance, so he took it upon himself to begin my training. Taking the time to outline his process to me would have only defeated his purpose.

Having no one to hold my hand forced me to take initiative on my own. In retrospect, I can truly appreciate his unorthodox approach to toughening me up. I think of it as his sink or swim method. Shortly after I erected the hoop set Manuel passed away, never having the chance to see me enjoy it. Just the same, he was always on my mind whenever I used it. In a way it felt as though he were still looking after me, only now he was doing it from behind my eyes.

Because my mother's life was anything but ordinary she often resorted to unconventional means to obtain loans. Banks weren't exactly sympathetic to her plight. That is where Menasco came in. He was our go-to guy for short-term loans. His first name was Paul, but my mom always referred to him by his last name, Menasco. He was tall and slender with an oversized, pitted nose that always had a reddish hue to it. Throw in a top hat and you'd have a lanky W.C. Fields.

His only companion was a cat named Squeaky who never showed affection toward anyone other than her beloved steward. During our visits Menasco would always sit on his leather recliner, Indian style, with a half-asleep Squeaky on his lap. Menasco liked to talk with his hands. One of his hands would be occupied with a beer while the other was free to wave about in the air.

Menasco was an alcoholic who, like Willy (the carpenter), was driven to drink by a tragic incident. While he and his wife were driving home one evening a drunk driver pulled into their lane from the opposite direction. The impact of the resulting head-on collision sent Menasco's wife through the windshield, decapitating her. Paul survived the accident but a part of him must have died with her that fateful night.

Like Manuel, Menasco grew up during the Great Depression. He often had to search for work on foot and those pursuits would often span several days. He did everything from working on oil rigs to delivering blocks of ice door-to-door. After acquiring enough money to support his siblings for a week or so he would return home. But soon the funds ran out and he would have to start his quest all over again.

When the Great Depression ended Menasco earned a college degree and acquired a position with the Federal Government. He somehow successfully maneuvered his way straight into retirement. When he had finally achieved a secure position in life, his refrigerator never went empty. In fact, his fridge had to be cleared out nearly every week owing to the mounds of uneaten food. My mom said his habitual hoarding stemmed from the extreme deprivation he had experienced as a kid. Fortunately, his eccentricity often provided us with a decent haul of groceries.

For the most part, Menasco was a happy drunk, but if anyone wanted anything from him it had to be on his terms. During one of our meetings a telemarketer called and Menasco immediately activated the speaker phone feature so that my mom and I could listen in. The representative began his spiel with, "Hello Mr. Menasco! How are you today?" Without a moment's hesitation he retorted, "I'm horny as hell! What can you do for me?" The ensuing dial tone from the other end signified the poor guy's abrupt surrender. Menasco believed that what someone else tells you isn't as important as your response to it. Perhaps in the hands of a highly competent salesperson that same call would have been an opportunity for growth (and a sale) rather than defeat.

Menasco also maintained that a person must always be in control of their circumstances and not the other way around. He elaborated by saying, "The easiest way to seize control of your circumstances is to dedicate yourself to a career that evokes an inner sense of passion. In doing so you will harness the power to navigate through even the roughest seas."

These visits were often a torturous affair for my mother, particularly because they often played out in the same fashion. She would call Menasco with a business idea that would prompt him to summon us to his house for further discussion. Once there, my mom and I would sit on the couch across from him while he proceeded to drink himself into oblivion. Eventually, he would even forget why we were there in the first place. We were then subjected to stories from his youth highlighting his struggles during the Great Depression.

On the bright side, these interludes put some temporary distance between us and our tattered house. Menasco's home was always cool in the summer and warm throughout the winter. Tolerating his inebriation was the price of admission and the temporary comfort wasn't always worth it. Most of those meetings ended with little more than a bag of groceries to show for our time. After all, we were merely catering to the whims of an alcoholic.

Fortunately, not all of my mentors were so callous. Dennis was a retired ventriloquist whom I met in an electronics outlet store while killing time, waiting for a movie matinee to start.

After wrapping up the purchase of a brand new computer, he stopped me to ask if I knew anything about setting them up. Seizing the opportunity to introduce myself as a handyman, I immediately offered to swing by after my matinee and set up his entire system. It was a deal sealed by a hearty hand shake.

The movie, by the way, was *The Hitchhiker's Guide to the Galaxy*. It's a story about an ordinary guy who's about to set out on the adventure of a lifetime, appropriate selection given the circumstances. After the movie, I made good on my promise and set up his new computer. The project took about an hour during which we got to know one another a little better. Dennis was big on crossword puzzles and Sherlock Holmes novels. As a result he had developed an extensive and equally impressive vocabulary. In fact, the first word he ever taught me was autodidact, meaning a self-taught person. Not only did I earn a new client but Dennis would also turn out to be a trustworthy friend and mentor.

Dennis began his career in show biz at the tender age of ten while trying his hand at magic. Unfortunately, that career choice never amounted to much. Then one day his father took him to a vaudeville show featuring a ventriloquist named Bob Evans who was performing his two-man act. While watching this amazing performance, Dennis knew he had found his calling. He would later leave his hometown of Oak Park, Illinois, and head straight for Hollywood.

According to Dennis, all professional ventriloquists have two things in common. They are all autodidactic and all learned their craft before the onset of puberty. There are no exceptions. In the early 19th century, ventriloquists were suspected of being in league with the devil. But a fellow by the name of Abbie De La Chapelle published a book back in 1772 titled, La Engostrome (the Greek word for ventriloquism). After extensive research, he concluded that ventriloquists were quite harmless.

Dennis had been performing as a professional ventriloquist since his early teens. During some of those performances he experienced a form of dissociation referred to as spontaneous schizophrenia. Because a ventriloquist is essentially pulling off a two-person comedy act, part of the brain is doing the ventriloquist while the other part is doing the dummy, so when a vent is really on a roll, occasionally the dummy or figure will say something the vent has not heard before. Consequently, the ventriloquist will react and laugh as though he were part of the audience. By Dennis' account, "It's a strange feeling to make yourself laugh with something you didn't know you knew."

Much of his entertainment career involved some of Hollywood's premiere elite and he often took pleasure in sharing fascinating accounts that included greats such as Lucille Ball, Judy Garland and Edger Bergen. He even had a hand in the making of Sir Anthony Hopkins' American film debut entitled, *Magic*. Ironically, it had very little to do with magic. Instead, the film was based on a novel (by the same name) about a ventriloquist who goes stark raving mad.

Dennis also worked as a director for a daytime news telecast and often boasted about being one of the first to witness the first lunar landing. On that historic day he was directing the live feed from space for the West Coast. As the astronauts approached the Moon's surface, Dennis had his hand positioned over the broadcast abort button. In the event that something should go wrong, he would immediately kill the feed. Fortunately, everything went according to plan and due to the time delay he got to witness a monumental piece of history a full eight seconds before the rest of the west coast. He was all about the little things.

When I once roamed the streets of Los Angeles, I often considered myself a triple threat because I couldn't find work as an actor, handyman or general laborer. It was during those lean years that Dennis welcomed me into his home with warm meals, great company and interesting stories. Stenciled over the doorway to his kitchen were the words, "Pilgrim on Earth, thy home is Heaven; stranger, thou art the guest of God." It's a passage from *Science and Health with Key to the Scriptures by Marry Baker Eddy*. Like my mother, Dennis was a firm believer in the teachings of the Church of Christ, Scientist.

Because my mother introduced me to several religious doctrines before committing herself to Christian Science, I never felt pressured to join the ranks and to this day continue to have no affiliation with any particular faith. Dennis also never pushed the church's ideology on me. Instead, he often made comparisons between his practice and other doctrines such as Buddhism. His favorite quote by Mary Baker Eddy was, "Stand guard at the portal of your mind." To reference a similar idea from Buddhism, he brought up something called *Samma Sati* which refers to right mindfulness. It suggests that one should become aware of his/her mind, feelings and body.

After having had the opportunity to meet my mother, Dennis became concerned that many of the beliefs I clung to weren't exactly my own. Still, he never once criticized her. On the contrary, he always spoke highly of her for doing such a fine job raising me. He added that, in one form or another, we all suffer from a bit of dissociation. My mother dissociated herself from a single identity to protect against childhood trauma. Dennis often dissociated himself from a single identity while entertaining crowds with his ventriloquism act. Similarly, never having committed myself to a single identity either, I managed to shift in and out of different personas to accommodate those around me. His final piece of advice to me was, "Stick with whatever works and continue building on it. There are no rules to this thing."

At the ripe age of eighty-two, Max was like my Obi Wan Kenobi. We were first introduced by a former landlord who often helped me find work as a handyman throughout Los Angeles. Being a long-time friend of Max's, she knew he always had multiple projects piling up around the house. It only made sense to connect the two of us. She also mentioned he was a wellspring of knowledge and would impart it whether I wanted it or not. Along with a decent wage, he would also be willing to supply me with an occasional meal, provided I could tolerate his company long enough. She cautioned that Max wasn't the easiest character to get along with. Still, it made little difference to me since I had a knack for getting along with just about anyone - or so I thought.

Over time, Max and I steadily became better acquainted. He turned out to be the type of person who took pleasure in micromanaging just about everyone in his life. He didn't trust most outsiders and I was no exception. While I worked on his lawn, Max would walk beside me and point out the weeds from the non-weeds because he didn't think I had enough sense to make the distinction myself. Attempting to convince him otherwise was an exercise in futility. I'd probably have an easier time herding cats. Max did, however, take an interest in helping determine what career path would best suit me.

During the Great Depression, Max owed much of his success to lucky breaks. During World War II he was drafted into the U.S. military. After serving in several capacities, he was deployed to the South Pacific. The war ended shortly thereafter, but Max remained in the military to take advantage of his educational benefits. As his studies progressed, so did his rank. Eventually

Max became a management analyst who served under several high ranking officers and was charged with drafting their letters and documents. Regarding his military career Max said, "If there was a mistake to be made, I made it, but learning from those mistakes was all the more important."

Max was the son of immigrants from London, England. His mother was functionally illiterate and his father was a master craftsman who specialized in making cabinets. Unable to afford an education for their child, they just left him to his own devices. Surrounding himself with books, he willfully taught himself to read. Learning to read unleashed and strengthened his ability to write. He also had a knack for drawing. Following his military career, he eventually found work as a cartoonist for a local paper. When it came to achieving success, Max never pushed any opportunity off the table.

His marriage lasted well over thirty-five years. The secret to the longevity of their relationship rested in her willingness to submit entirely to him. Unfortunately, she passed away before I could meet her. She was apparently a huge fan of pink and white color combinations, so as a memorial to her, Max planted a rose bush in one of their flower beds that bore corresponding blooms every spring. The blossoms gave Max the sense that his beloved was still with him. As winter approached, he would say his goodbyes and await her return in the spring.

Max came to know a lot about my childhood and the dysfunction therein. He admitted to never having met anyone as meek as me before. To him, I was like a lion that lacked any awareness of his own brute strength. After meeting my mother he concluded that my transformation would take place once I learned to distance myself from her. He cautioned that obsessing over money would only hinder my chances of ever obtaining it.

I read a book entitled, *How to think like Leonardo Da Vinci.* Its author describes some of the characteristics of this highly accomplished individual. For example, whenever Leonardo painted he would set up a barrier between himself and the canvas so that the light from the candle would illuminate the canvas without his shadow getting in the way. This simple practice is what allowed the radiance of his genius to shine forth.

In many ways, I was completely unlike Leonardo Di Vinci. My faulty habits, thoughts, and beliefs went unchecked for years and continually intruded in all of my endeavors, only to sabotage them. Max recognized that a hunger for money could potentially be my undoing, so he began going to work on me. He firmly believed in something called a *quid pro quo*, a Latin phrase meaning, "this for that."

At first, I thought he chose this method of payment just to save himself some cash, but he had another goal in mind. Nevertheless, without a financial incentive to drive me, I resorted to cutting corners, but such behavior wasn't about to fly with Max. If I couldn't learn to deliver quality work on a *quid pro quo* basis, then sweetening the deal with cash wasn't going to make much difference. He believed there was a crucial distinction between working for money and committing one's self to a meaningful undertaking. According to Max, money was just a means to an end. Real dividends came from purpose-driven work.

Anytime I said something couldn't be done he would devise a clever solution to ultimately prove me wrong. If ever I brought up money woes he would propose a money-making scheme and challenge me to act on it. Even so, I rarely put forth any genuine interest in seeing it through. Who has time to formulate business ideas when something as effortless as complaining is at your disposal? Dodging liability seemed to complement my other favorite pastime of drifting off into the clouds. That was precisely why Max saw fit to be a total pain in the ass with me. Furthermore, thanks to his astute observations, he was able to hone in on many of my weaknesses.

How did I become so aloof to begin with? Whatever happened to that resilient kid who had endured a harsh existence with a psychologically unstable mother? What happened to the passion that once drove that same kid to sell miscellaneous items door-to-door just to earn money to help pay utilities? Moreover, how was I ever going to get anywhere in life with success my goal but defeat in my thoughts? Was I merely looking for handouts these days? Max had an acronym that summarized his thoughts on the matter. He called it T.A.N.S.T.A.A.F.L., which stood for, "There Ain't No Such Thing As A Free Lunch."

After observing my behavior for a few days it became apparent to him that I had an excuse for just about everything. Then again, he also recognized how one of my mother's personalities used her shortcomings to evoke pity and get her own way. But Max wasn't one to buck-pass and proved it by blazing his own trail. Even though her faulty behaviors would have had me chasing my tail for years, Max would have never offered his assistance had I come across as averse to personal growth. In some weird way, having Max point out the root causes of my inadequacies seemed to loosen their stranglehold on me.

Max turned out to be a devoted fan and supporter of mine because he was able to see the potential in me long before I could recognize it in myself. He also felt particularly optimistic about my interest in writing a book someday. One *quid pro quo* he worked out for me entailed writing letters to various people in his inner circle. After proofreading each one, he confessed that there might be a future for me in writing after all. Nonetheless,

Max wasn't the type of person to just tell you something could be done; he had to go out and prove it.

While rounding his eighty-eighth birthday, Max was putting the finishing touches on his own book idea. He called it, "The Parabolic Masqueraders" and quoted Woody Allen as saying, "Eighty percent of success is showing up." He believed that the key to success was just getting started. His tenacity would then act as a powerful magnet to attract the people and conditions that can turn a dream into reality.

When Max began work on his book he didn't know the first thing about getting it published. Instead, he focused the majority of his time and energy on just the writing aspect. Like Dennis, Max had a vocabulary that would knock your socks off. The evidence for it could be found throughout all the pages of his novel. Once he had completed his preliminary draft, he employed his skills as a cartoonist to work out the cover.

Unfortunately, his hands weren't as steady as they once were, so he turned to the internet for help. After an extensive search he came across some illustrations by an artist who lived in New Mexico. He then contacted the artist to express interest in one of her works for the cover of his book. Impressed by his sheer determination, she donated the illustration for free and referred him to a self-publishing company specializing in first-time authors. As an expression of his gratitude, Max decided to dedicate the book to the artist. This unlikely collaboration serves as a testament to his unwavering belief in the law of attraction, which is essentially a belief that "like attracts like."

Chapter II:

The Rite Stuff

Modeling personal behaviors after those of mythological heroes has aided in elevating my consciousness toward a spiritual level. The giving of one's compassion toward others is a trait shared by numerous folk heroes. This mode of behavior is what ultimately opens them up to their latent spiritual nature. Conversely, animal nature is a means of existence where self-interest or self-preservation is the primary concern. Movies tend to portray the bad guy as one whose primary focus is on self-enrichment by any means necessary. Their selfish desires often lead them to act out like animals. On the other hand, the good guys tend to champion causes greater than or other than themselves. In so doing they overcome overwhelming odds for the good of the many, even at the cost of their own lives.

Catching myself slipping toward the *dark side* is a never-ending affair. But maintaining a sense of gratitude for my defeats as well as the triumphs has better aligned me with the natural flow of life. This new sense of harmony which stabilizes one between the darkness and the light allows me to not assign blame whenever I find myself in unfavorable circumstances. Besides, should I truly hold anyone else accountable for the many tragedies in my life that later turned out to be successes in the making?

Mantras and meditations have aided me in maintaining this heroic sense of self. One such mantra is, "Thank you for granting me this dynamic, vibrant, healthy, strong body that I enjoy. Thank you for every day, in every way, making me better and better, happier and happier, healthier and healthier and stronger and stronger. And thank you for granting me a mind that is open to everything and attached to nothing." This is what I refer to as my attitude of gratitude.

When it became evident that my acting career was on life support, I began working as a handyman for two brothers who owned and operated their own real estate management company. They would send me from one apartment complex to another to carry out all sorts of odd jobs. Over time I managed to earn a level of camaraderie with them that allowed me to vent about personal issues, my living situation being one of them. My landlord was taking full advantage of my carpentry skills without granting any sort of remuneration. So any humble abode would be a step up from the corner in which I managed to paint myself.

The only prospect the brothers could suggest was a small office space located on one of their properties. It was basically a room equipped with a sink, toilet and shower that measured a total of 150 square feet and was situated in a corner of an underground parking garage beneath a four-story building. Without a moment's hesitation I jumped at the offer and after hammering out a suitable lease, that miniature Van Nuys studio became my new home. Priced at three hundred a month, my rent included water and electricity, making it an even bigger steal. Admittedly, living in the heart of earthquake country added an element of anxiety to the whole deal because one decent tremor would pretty much put an end to my story. Nevertheless, that pint-sized castle proved to be a safe haven for my story to continue uninterrupted.

My new digs were once used as an office for the on-site property manager. But because he had already set up an adjacent room as his office, my room was turned into storage space. I remember the first time it was shown to me. Since 150 square feet isn't a lot of ground to cover, the whole tour only took a matter of seconds. The carpet was made from a cheap grade of commercial material. It was also soiled with oil and grease stains, as if someone had once stored old engine parts on it.

Off to the right of the entrance was a three-by-five-foot window looking out onto a small concrete patio, made private by a wooden fence running along the rear of the complex. If someone on the outside wanted to sneak a peek through my one window they would need to get on all fours to do so. That was because my studio was built eight feet below ground level and the window had to be positioned as close to the ceiling as possible. As a result, the bottom frame of my window was at eye-level with the grass outside.

To the immediate left of the entry door was the bathroom. A wall with a doorway separated it from the main living area. Entering the bathroom, the sink was located to the left and the toilet to the right with the two facing one another. A large square mirror was affixed to the wall behind the sink, making that tiny corridor appear slightly larger than it actually was. Opposite the wall behind the toilet was the shower located at the farthest left corner of the room.

The ceiling measured roughly seven feet in height. The actual height of the ceiling was eight feet but a faux ceiling was constructed to hide the plumbing that serviced the apartment above. It was made from those ceiling tiles commonly used in office settings - the kind that people throw their pencils into when bored. Every time the upstairs neighbor flushed or ran a faucet the sound of cascading water would pass along my ceiling and continue down the side of the wall. Believe it or not, this daily occurrence provided a feeling of tranquility to the place.

Fortunately, it didn't take much to furnish my underground cave. My full-sized bed alone dramatically reduced the remaining available living area. After adding a desk, stool and mini-fridge to the decor, my bachelor pad was pretty much complete. It just needed my professional touch to make it a home. Besides, living within four dingy white walls with rustic carpeting got old real fast, so why not personalize it a little? I struck a deal with my new landlords requiring me to purchase $300 worth of building materials, just enough to refinish my studio from top to bottom. In exchange, they agreed to knock off a month of rent. It was a win-win scenario. Their property would be renovated without any additional labor costs and I would no longer have to dwell in a make-shift cavern. Well, it would still be a cavern, but a cavern with a facelift.

Soon the oil stained, commercial-grade carpet was replaced with laminate flooring and the walls were treated to fresh paint and custom-fitted baseboards. Even the bathroom would undergo a facelift. One afternoon I came upon a lamp set out by the curb as rubbish. It just stood there beaming with potential, so naturally I had to take it home to make the necessary modifications. With a little tweaking, this discarded artifact soon became the centerpiece of my bathroom ceiling. It looked like something out of a contemporary art studio. More importantly, it hung as mute proof that one man's trash is another man's ceiling fixture.

The ceiling tiles that once masked the suspended plumbing overhead were removed, giving me that extra foot of headroom. An extra foot may not seem like much, but in a small space every square inch counts. Rather than hiding the plumbing, I chose to showcase it by painting it and the concrete slab overhead in white. That approach appeared to miraculously expand the dimensions of the studio.

This studio didn't seem like much at the start. But enhancing the overall look of my living quarters unleashed its greater potential. Had I opted to leave it in the same condition I acquired it, I would have been forfeited an opportunity to experience personal growth. This is essentially what journeys are all about. In choosing to look past superficial appearances, a hero comes to recognize and utilize the potential gifts inherent within. What once appeared to be tragic experiences in my past were merely the preparatory steps necessary for overcoming the challenges that lay ahead. My success in transforming my little nest marked a new turning point in my journey.

The apartment complex was located close to a gym where I spent much of my down time. Also nearby was a park where I could walk in circles to either think, to kill time, or even think of new ways to kill more time. In the span of those three years only one fellow tenant ever learned of my existence down below. She would use the parking garage as her designated smoking area so her apartment wouldn't reek of cigarettes. Apart from our casual association, I made a habit of keeping to myself so that no others were aware of my presence. This allowed my little corner of the world to remain somewhat sacred. It represented a quiet center where I could insulate myself from the world's struggles.

Shortly after I took up residence in my underground dungeon, the once spectacular Los Angeles housing bubble began to deflate. It soon became apparent that steady handyman work was about to become a thing of the past. Even the brothers I relied heavily upon for work were starting to feel the strain from the dwindling economy. Conserving resources, they assigned any available work to their senior laborers.

My other regular clients exhausted most of the equity in their homes, leaving little remaining for remodeling or repairs. My handyman business started to suffer and I too soon felt the strain in my own finances. The most affordable meals I could find were weight-loss shakes. I discovered that three cans per day contained enough essential nutrients to sustain me. Of course this diet worked as advertised and caused my waistline to shrink rather quickly. As far as my acting career was concerned, the background was the only part of the set where I could find work.

Each month prompted the routine of pleading for a rent extension from my landlords. Even though they never had a problem granting a postponement, facing them each month with insufficient funds never got any easier. Fortunately, I had some elderly friends who always set aside work to keep me busy. They would also offer me an occasional hot meal, a welcome relief from diet shakes. Regardless, I continued to falter on both work and rent money. I had arrived at rock bottom, both figuratively and literally. In the wake of events, I did in fact reside in an underground garage studio.

Any money I earned immediately went to back rent. Recreation was reduced to a daily walk around the park or a trip to the gym. Being totally broke enabled me to realize that free forms of entertainment were among the finest privileges one could ever know. Among my meager possessions was a DVD series titled, "Joseph Campbell and The Power of Myth." At one time Joseph Campbell was one of the world's foremost authorities on the subject of mythology and near the end of his life he completed the *Power of Myth* series with Bill Moyers at Skywalker Ranch.

I came to know this series through my mother who had come upon it by chance at a local library. When she saw someone was turning in a VHS version of the series she decided to give it a go. Even though she had never heard of Joseph Campbell, his insights would soon provide her with clues related to the transformation of consciousness. As a kid I would sit beside her and watch that series of interviews. Unable to fully comprehend their meaning, I was still able to enjoy Joe's enthusiasm for the subject of which he appeared to be so knowledgeable. The mythological stories he related enthralled me to no end. Through his telling of fables I was left feeling as though he were a grandfatherly presence dispensing age-old wisdom.

His advice to anyone wishing to conjure their own creative spirit was to designate a sacred place where one could remain uninterrupted from outside distractions. This room or space should be devoid of any links to one's personal or social obligations, such as family or work. More importantly, this space should be utilized for a treasured pastime which utterly evokes one's overwhelming sense of joy. I took this advice to heart and applied it to my underground man cave. A major component in my remodeling project involved the use of distinct color schemes for the purpose of inspiring creativity at home.

The walls in the main living area were painted beige to symbolize calm and simplicity. A dark shade of brown was applied to the baseboards throughout. Brown symbolizes such characteristics as stability, reliability, comfort and endurance. It also added a sense of earthiness to the space. Because the bathroom was the smallest area in the studio, it required a color that could give it some impact. The solution was a synthesis of yellow and orange. The combined symbology of these two colors added just the right amount of depth to my spatially challenged lavatory. Yellow represents energy, balance, enthusiasm and warmth, whereas orange suggests optimism, idealism, imagination and hope. When the world outside chewed me up and spit me out, this sacred space would serve to revitalize my spirits.

A friend gave me a housewarming gift which was like a metaphorical bottle of Champaign to christen the project. It was a narrow picture frame with one word painted on the canvas in red, vertically-aligned letters - *Simplify*. Considering it to be a sign of ultra-significance, I hung it on the bathroom wall, centered on the entryway. So positioned, those big red letters could be seen from just about any angle in the studio. Not only does the color red symbolize all things intense and passionate, every letter would serve to remind me of the most important principle applicable to any endeavor - keep it simple, stupid!

During my high school career I read about an ancient battle where the offensive force set out across an ocean to claim a new territory. However, as their ships drew closer to land, it became apparent how vastly outnumbered they were. As a result, many of the men could not conceive of victory. Sensing doubt among the ranks, the commanding admiral gave the order to incinerate their own ships after dropping anchor. The admiral's order really drove the point home for his soldiers standing on the brink of battle. By destroying their only means of retreat, failure to achieve their goal was no longer an option. With no available means for withdrawal, they managed to march toward victory.

My underground studio offered little means of escape from the fact that I had become destitute. Metaphorically speaking, my journey to Los Angeles was an attempt to conquer a foreign territory where the odds were clearly stacked against me. Similarly, I was forced to root out whatever factors were responsible for bringing me to my knees. It is said that when we lose everything we are free to try anything. Perhaps writing held the clues to unlock my own transformation. What's more, just before my departure from Texas a friend handed me a journal with a hand written inscription on the inside cover. It read, "To Alex for your journeys." But despite the journey I had already undergone just to get to Los Angeles, its pages would remain blank for several more years. Then one day I was suddenly struck with the impulse to begin journaling in it.

This impulse wasn't driven by chance. On the contrary, it was the direct result of incorporating ritual back into my life. Rituals were first introduced to me at home. Saying grace before every meal was intended to create a sense of gratitude for having food on the table. Actually, having any food at all was a kind of daily miracle back then. Cleaning house every weekend was another ritual that involved listening to classical music to help ease us through the day. Our mother was a firm believer in the power of prayer. Her ritual involved the two of us holding hands and reciting prayers in unison. Perhaps this was to let God know that we were all on the same page.

According to Joseph Campbell, introducing ritual into any creative endeavor allows the transcendent to shine through the veil of temporality. Just what is the transcendent? No one can truly know because that which is transcendent is unknowable. It can't be named or even logically understood thereby rendering it a total mystery. The only way to truly comprehend transcendence is through an "ah hah" moment, an experience whereby a piece of music, art, text or ritual grabs hold of you in a way that transcends words or explanation.

By participating in a sound ritual one can come into accord with this mystery realm. Why the importance of connecting with the mystery dimension? Because anything that isn't rooted to its source will lack the essential nourishment to co-exist with its environment. The ritual that inspired me to write always took place at night. Since everything comes out of darkness and returns back into it I figured that nighttime was an ideal period from which to draw inspiration. In the early stages of my creative writing, the initial product was both vague and nebulous. But nothing is ever in its final state because everything in existence is either being or becoming. In realizing this I began to recognize my ideas shift around on paper until a clear and concise thought was ultimately formulated. This important realization made it possible for me to see the transcendent radiating through all things.

For instance, consider the following. My underground dungeon wasn't just some room comprised of four walls. It was a living, breathing space that girdled my private life. That is why every color choice was the product of careful study and reflection. The Greeks in particular understood the importance of breathing life into their structures through innovative engineering techniques. The Greek Parthenon is more than just an ancient ruin.

The Parthenon has "optical refinements" built into its structure that produce physiological and psychological effects which are not geometrical in nature. These refinements were intended to offset the presence of optical illusions. For example, each of the columns in the Parthenon was built with a slight bulge in the middle, to make them appear "straight". With that said, you won't find any true right angles or straight lines in its construction. Not only does this feature illustrate stress and tension on each pillar supporting the weight of the roof, but in a mythological sense, every pillar supports the ideals housed within the Parthenon – balance and beauty.

Even though my studio was no Parthenon, it still needed to embody a metaphorical womb where renewal could take place on a daily basis. So one might see how the original dingy white walls just weren't going to cut it for me. And because that studio was to be my own sacred sanctuary, every element added to it would have to transcend its practical function. In other words, paint was more than just paint to me. Every color represented a frequency from which I could draw strength and inspiration. In a sense, my color selections didn't merely decorate the walls - they added meaning to every surface. Without personal significance, a beige wall would just be another boring beige wall.

You might say that renovating that studio into a temple of sorts made it an ideal place to practice ritual. The importance of ritual is that it reenacts a myth. By participating in a ritual, one is participating in a myth. And what is that myth? It can be any activity that puts one into accord with the mysterious source of life. For me, entering my home was like entering a chapel. When it came to earning a living, the outside world could often evoke the worst in me. But entering this private sanctuary reestablished a sense of solace that always waited for me beyond my front door. It is within those four walls that I could listen to the music that inspired me or watch the documentaries that shifted my psychological perspective.

My nighttime ritual consisted of three congruent activities. One diversion involved watching Joseph Campbell interviews many times over to achieve a better understanding of mythology in general. The other undertaking involved journaling the various thoughts and ideas impressed upon me during each viewing. One final component contributed greatly to my understanding and appreciation for the material. I found that smoking a controlled dose of *cannabis* beforehand helped to prevent trivial distractions from fragmenting my already scattered attention span. With my mind finally at ease, the information became far easier to assimilate.

This ritual was initiated by the lighting of a large white candle sitting atop a four-foot high, cast iron candelabrum positioned in a corner of my room. I could easily see it from the bathroom floor where my ritual would play out. Once lit, the candle would cast a luminescent, bust-like figure onto the wall. This radiant figure didn't manifest overnight. It was rather the product of at least a week of candle burning. Over time the flame slowly melted away the candle's outer rim, resulting in the projection of a gleaming effigy.

I felt that anointing it with a name synonymous with wisdom might actually invoke the spirit which brought such character into my humble abode. So I went with Marcus Aurelius. In life, Marcus Aurelius was a Roman emperor who was known as the philosopher king. It was he who said, "Dig within. Within is the wellspring of Good; and it is always ready to bubble up, if you just dig." I was indeed digging deep in the hopes of rediscovering the good in life. In reality, I understood that the figure on the wall was likely pure happenstance. But that distinct shape symbolized something far more significant. I interpreted it to mean that all of my inward searching was about to pay off.

On the third night of performing this ritual, something seemingly miraculous and a bit ominous started happening to me. While listening to one of Joseph Campbell's many mythological stories, I was suddenly overtaken with a succession of insights that raced through my mind. It seemed appropriate to inscribe them in the journal for future analysis. My excited hands started writing as quickly as they could manage. The first thought to make impact was, "Your work is to discover your work and then with all your heart, give yourself to it!" The next sequence of revelations followed immediately thereafter:

- There is no meaning to life. There is only the experience of life. Meanings are subject to interpretations and interpretations are subject to even more interpretation.

- Respect all life forms. Mother Earth has provided ample food and drink for all. We along with all other life forms are subject to consumption on some level by one another. All organisms must live harmoniously together for mutual advantage.

- Never resist. Always allow in peace and understanding.

- Male and female are merely the vessels through which to bring about new life. Children belong to the planet and not to us. We are simply the temporal guardians charged with the honor of sharing and nurturing the experience of life with these new manifestations of life. We must all do our part to ensure the survival of life on this planet until she herself returns to her source to be reborn anew.

- The sun only shines on the hemisphere of the Earth which is exposed to its light. Yet the moon rises in the dark of night to reflect the sun's radiance so that it will remind those cast unto the darkness that they are never without illumination. This is the light of truth.

- The word *being* implies that it cannot be reduced to a finite entity. *Being* is constant and cannot exist in the past or future. We must submit to *being* and die to our past daily. This is the only way we will evolve together as one.

- Honor your past, don't relive it. This way you will be eternally free from an identity defined by your perception of the past.

- Always respect one another. What you do to your brother/sister, you do to yourself.

- The phrase *I Am* represents the ultimate state of presence or being. Be careful in choosing whatever follows these words. For those words might then become your God.

- To find God, simply be aware of your own presence. Exist in a state of *being* where time and space are void. That is where you will find your center and realize that you and the center are one. God and you are one. Never place God outside yourself. That will become your fall from grace.

- When your center is discovered, you will realize that you are like a beam of light emitting from a brilliant sphere of purity. You and the sphere are one. This is why true happiness exists only in the experience of *being* alive.

- Honor the journey that will one day become your past. The destination is always secondary. Harbor an ever-present sense of eternal (constant) gratitude for the chance to be a human who is a reflection of the grace of God.

- Time and space equate to illusion. Dismiss time and space and you end all illusion.

- You all are God. One sphere, one planet, one sky, one body of water, one country landscaped with an array of one people. United as one, protect and honor the Earth. She is the home for your present experience. Love and cherish her. She is your blessed mother.

- Never again fear the word *death*. It is only a signpost to the one true constant called change. Death is merely the changing of one form into another. Therein lies the cycle of life. Your death sustains the life essence of whatever it submits to. In part, your death becomes the catalyst for life itself. Say *Yes* to life!

- Anyone who takes a life out of greed takes his own. Life force must never take; it must always submit. This is why the dead must be honored for they merely change into the air you breathe, the sun that warms you, the water that cools you and that land that sustains you.

- Your true state of *being* is the present moment.

- Science and religion are one. Religion is the history of the study of science and science is the study of the history of religion.

- Whatever you think the acquisition of wealth will give you (aliveness, peace, self-esteem) reflects the qualities you must first develop in order to become more magnetic to money and abundance. The process of getting there reflects your state of being.

- I am that stranger who has nothing to offer you but is telling you to look inside.

After the last of these epiphanies had filtered in, I sat in awe of what had transpired. Because the whole thing was difficult to process, I was inclined to stop trying altogether. However, what it left me with was a sense of potentiality brewing from within. Sadly, the wonder of it all didn't last very long. The wonder was soon supplanted by feelings of fear and paranoia. It was reminiscent of my very first day of school. Everything appeared to be kosher with my mom at my side, but the moment she left the nightmare began. But even that experience, like the one unfolding before me, was prelude to a grander escapade.

At that point in the evening, the high from my ritualistic smoking session had already worn off, making everything that followed seem purely natural and not drug-induced. The only logical means to combat the rising terror was to lie down and fall asleep in the hope of waking to the light of day as soon as possible. The moment I closed my eyes it felt as though my body had somehow disengaged itself. Then numerous thoughts began to inundate my consciousness, but these were unlike any of my previous insights. First, a problematic scenario would pop up, followed by an immediate solution. It was as though my mind was playing good cop/bad cop with itself, only I had no interest in being held captive to its restless pattern of fluctuating reflections. Nevertheless, these troubling thoughts sped up to a dizzying speed in what felt like a instant.

Without having the sense of a body to lift out of bed, I was completely at the mercy of a tortured mind. This must be what

Hell is like. It wasn't a landscape of red molten lava, bursting with flames and governed by some horned demon. It was far worse. I was trapped in total darkness with only an endless cycle of thoughts to accompany me. But I also got the impression that these thoughts were not an absolute representation of what reality has to be. Besides, if I were generating these thoughts, who was the one observing their tortured effects? Apparently, that little observation was all it took to bring the vertigo to a sudden end.

The experience that ensued was so extraordinary that I can still vividly recall it to this day. What had been a frantic hell only a moment prior was now the most profound sense of peace I had ever felt in my life. It was beyond beautiful. If multiplicity were to suddenly transmute into unification, this sensation would have been the result. That's the closest I've ever come to expressing it in words that always fall short of the actual experience. Just saying that peace surrounded me simply would not suffice because in that moment I was peace or perhaps it was me. Either way, there was only sublime stillness and it was truly magnificent.

One might think that event alone might signify the final stage of this whirlwind experience, but not so. Another (what I think of as) critical occurrence began to unfold. It felt as though the one was steadily dividing into the many thus bringing the sense of the body, along with the bed it rested upon, back into being. Then I thought to myself, "If I allow myself to give in to this experience again, it might turn out to be a one way trip." In a flash I was faced with two options - fade back into that blissful state or resist it. The possibility of being one with everything rested on the one hand while the fear of ceasing to exist entirely sat on the other.

I literally felt as though the first option was a precursor to imminent death. But if I were merely yielding to the inevitable, why not give it a go? Earlier that evening I had been listening to a lecture by Joseph Campbell concerning self-sacrifice. In it he referenced the Native Americans who charged General Custer shouting, "It is a great day to die!" They clearly weren't afraid of letting go. And with that my thinking was reoriented from a position of surrender to one of courage, thus prompting my decision to fade back in.

One might think that I would have at least gotten out my list of phone numbers to start making final goodbye calls in the dead of night. But that wasn't the case. All of my obligations and commitments to the world had suddenly fallen away. The only gesture of good will (you might say) that I performed that night was to un-lock my front door. Why? Because if someone were to come looking for me they would have no problem getting in to discover the body. Even in death, the last thing I would ever want was to make another person's life more difficult than it had to be.

Unlocking that front door was symbolic of setting all fear aside. After peering around the room that had doubled as my sanctuary, I lay back down and closed my eyes one last time. What was once a womb had now become my tomb.

In mythology the tomb is merely the preliminary venue for an inevitable resurrection. Opening my eyes to the dawn marked a kind of spiritual rebirth. And to ensure that it wasn't all just a dream I immediately got up and rushed toward the door which had, in fact, been unlocked. That door was never left unlocked. It didn't matter which side of it I was on; it was somewhat of a tic of mine.

Something else also dawned on me. The person who had slipped away in the night was not the same person who awoke the following morning. The sensory overload of my awakening that morning was awe inspiring. I was in perfect rapture with everything in existence. This feeling permeated every one of my senses. Sounds were sharper, images crisper and thoughts, although fewer, were keener. My every ensuing action was driven by instinct.

In one of his many lectures, Joseph Campbell highlights the term, *aesthetic arrest*. He is quoted as saying, "The aesthetic experience is a simple beholding of the object....you experience a radiance. You are held in aesthetic arrest." This radiance is regarded as the hidden power behind the world, transmitting itself through some physical form. The experience I had only the night before could be said to have been a kind of psychological rebirth. Along with this birth came the potential to reinvent myself in new and exciting ways. I liken the experience to what a newborn infant might feel when gazing in wonder at all it beholds for the first time.

For nearly two weeks all my attention was keenly focused on the present moment. Wherever I roamed, random strangers would stare at me with an inquisitive gaze, but only a few were inclined to probe further. When asked what was behind the sparkle in my eye, the only sensible thing to say was, "It's my birthday!" That wasn't entirely a lie, especially the way I felt at the precise moment my eyes focused on the sunbeams piercing through the blinds on the morning of what could only be described as a new lease on life.

I contend that birthdays don't have to commemorate only a physical birth. In fact, there's another event that I consider to be just as significant as the date printed on my birth certificate. It involved legally changing my last name only a few years after the big move to Los Angeles. Because my mother had such a severe distaste for the name Minharez, much of her hostility was focused on me simply for being born under it. However, she bore no malevolence toward my middle name, Demetrius. Perhaps it's because that was the one aspect of my birth she could control.

Throughout the duration of her pregnancy with me, my mother would pray incessantly for help in any possible form. With no memory and a severe, debilitating mental illness, she felt the only potential source of support available to her was divine intervention. So she interpreted my birth as a response from above providing the very help for which she had been pleading. Even at birth, great expectations had already been set for me. The middle name she bestowed upon me was Demetrius. As the story goes, she wanted to name me after the man who helped Jesus carry the cross. Later she discovered that a man named Simon had, in fact, helped with the cross, but by then the ink on my birth certificate had long since dried.

In the Bible, Demetrius was a silversmith who earned his living crafting silver idols of the Greek goddess, Artemis. She was viewed as a mother goddess associated with fertility. Some ancient inscriptions portray her as one who answers prayer, is acclaimed a savior, has lordship over supernatural powers, and has some power over fate. And as fate would have it, my mom opted to retain Demetrius over Simon. After all, I was literally considered to be the answer to her prayers. No pressure, indeed.

As far as a career in acting is concerned, having a name that can stick in the mind of a casting director can't hurt. So, in an attempt to give my headshot more impact, I played around with my name a bit. I tried prints showing my name in two ways - Alexander Minharez and Alexander Demetrius Minharez, but neither seemed to help my cause. Right around that same time I had also begun reading a book about the life of Michelangelo. Before starting his work on the statue of David, it was said that he could already see the masterpiece hidden within the stone. In essence, the only achievement for which he took credit was chipping away the excess stone to reveal the work of art within.

The words, "chipping away the excess," really struck a chord with me. Was holding onto the sentimentality associated with the Minharez name really necessary, especially when a name like Demetrius could be put to better use? This simple yet profound idea stirred me into action and after a bit of research and some modest legal fees, I found myself born anew. The official name change took place during the month of May, coincidentally the season when the Earth's northern hemisphere is tilted slightly more toward the sun. It was the auspiciousness of the season that gave me faith that my decision to let go of the past would somehow bring forth brighter days.

CHAPTER III:

A Write of Passage

It can truly be said that nothing ever goes wrong in my life. Everything unfolds just as it should. This perception grants me the patience to refrain from cursing my shortcomings. Only then have I found it feasible to conceive of solutions to life's little complications. It is when I start to perceive events as unfortunate that my ability to think in the affirmative is severely compromised. This is usually a sign that my victim identity is getting the better of me.

Victims tend to meditate on what they lack rather than what they already possess. Therefore, taking on the role of a victim casts me out of the light and into the darkness. To counter this I have found it extremely helpful to take a lesson from the sun above. Any portion of Earth turned away from the sun's light is automatically shadowed by darkness. However, because the sun does not carry a shadow in itself, it can only radiate light. So when the sun sets, it is only us who are cast into darkness. By identifying with the sun, I am reminded to always be a vehicle for the light.

Eastern religions promote the idea of releasing expectation from outcome. In doing so, one releases the associated burden of despair which allows the radiance of truth to permeate through any situation. Expectation is typically centered around probability. And in my experience, meditating on probability opens the possibility of a problematic life. It took the experience of being rooted in the present, even if just for a little while, for me to realize this. But it also takes a bit of courage to stay present, especially when I am so afraid. Nonetheless, courage is not the opposite of fear. Courage is acting in the face of fear.

It is courage that separates the folk hero from the ordinary citizen. Heroes are known for avoiding the routine or familiar path in order to discover all that has yet to be achieved. Similarly, it was Einstein who said, "The problems of the mind will never be solved at the level of the mind." He recognized that the mind often hinders one's ability to resolve problems by posing countless more. Likewise, I always had a hard time understanding most spiritual teachings or concepts due to all the restless chatter going on inside my head. So I took Einstein's sage observation and discovered a way to circumnavigate the mind. It involved a particular hallucinogen known for taking people to new heights.

Many diverse cultures use hallucinogens ritualistically to bring about profound insights. These insights help them to better understand their role in the natural order of things. Remaining in accord with their environment means staying rooted in being. For example, Native Americans performed rituals to align their actions with the needs of Nature herself. After all, they viewed the Earth as their sacred mother upon whom they were dependent for life itself. So they performed rituals to honor the animals whose lives were surrendered in service to the tribe. In their philosophy, the animal was superior to man and should be respected as such.

My brief experimentation with drugs helped to bring about certain insights that ultimately struck a balance between the needs of a restless mind an aching heart. After all, the mind isn't always interested in what the heart desires or even needs for that matter. But having achieved this balance, the dynamics of both could interact harmoniously without one dominating the other. Syncing these two dimensions was the key to restoring the peace that had been missing in my life for so long.

Pot was the first drug that notably made me aware of an inner consciousness, a consciousness like that of the sun, always emitting light even in the midst of total darkness. But without the use of a sound ritual to temper the experience, marijuana could just as easily become another means of escape. By incorporating a ritualistic use of the drug, the experience broadened my view of life just enough to witness an askew version of reality. The end result was a heightened ability to think outside the box. In fact, it almost eliminated the box altogether. After it had served its purpose to achieve an enhanced level of consciousness, I steadily phased pot out of my life. And because the levels of clarity I achieved were so remarkable, it appeared that excessive usage became more of a hindrance than a aid.

While epiphanies can be realized without the use of hallucinogens, the challenge remains the same - quieting the mind. The method of achieving this feat is completely up to the individual. In my case, there were no spiritual gurus around to show me the path to an elevated level of consciousness. If there were, the socialite crowd I hung with exhibited little interest in spiritual enlightenment. So when in Hollywood . . .

My experience with drugs can be broken into two distinct periods. The first could be called the free-wheeling stage. At this point in the game I was simply appeasing old curiosities and having a rip-roaring good time. The other phase involved gaining a deeper understanding as well as appreciation for the overall benefits of marijuana in particular. Fortune would also have it that both of these periods would not pass without the guidance of a seasoned veteran and friend.

Dana was the very first friend I ever made in Los Angeles. We worked together as hosts for the same restaurant, but after closing she took charge of showing me the ropes around town. Dana also had a real knack for talking to people. In fact, within the first half-hour or so of entering a bar, everyone inside would be eating right out of her hot little hand. This gift was credited to a technique she called *two degrees of separation.* The idea was to approach anyone with a series of statements or questions that might reveal a common bond between the two of you.

For example, she could start out by asking the other's opinion about an event that made recent headlines. The more general the event, the greater the potential for a broader range of possible answers and responses. She wanted the other person to reflect rather than react. Once she grabbed at something that put the other on common ground, she would probe a bit further to unveil a second degree of commonality. Dana encouraged me to draw parallels between the most trivial of occurrences because in her mind there is always something that unites one person with another. Even if the only common denominators one could find were 46 chromosomes and bipedal locomotion, use them.

Aside from being an incidental life coach, Dana also made a great wing-woman. Unlike the traditional wing-man, her tactics presented a new dynamic in the art of picking up girls. Our mutual enjoyment in the company of beautiful women, coupled with her capacity to engage any make or model into enticing conversation, rendered most subjects easy prey. If I happened to take notice of a girl, Dana would chat her up and then ask, "Oh by the way, have you met my dear friend Alex standing over there?" Like bowling pins, she would set 'em up and I would knock 'em down. And because Dana had a talent for making people feel as though they were the center of the universe they would often propose just about anything in return.

Several who had been pulled into Dana's gravitational sphere would gladly invite us to their homes for the proverbial after-party. Our nocturnal adventures took us to all four corners of greater Los Angeles. Some evenings we might find ourselves at a stunning Mulholland estate overlooking the canyon. Other times we might end up on the shores of Santa Monica. But whatever the location or occasion, our hosts routinely offered up drugs as a traditional means of breaking the ice among new friends.

Our favorite watering hole was a bar called "Birds" over in Hollywood. Metaphorically speaking, this bar was the woods, Dana was the bloodhound and I was the guy in the flannel jacket holding her leash. The moment we entered the bar I simply unleashed the hound; she took care of the rest. Because Dana was such a snake charmer, it was inevitable that a random stranger would extend another auspicious, after-party invite.

Cocktails were another useful tool for stilling the mind. And what is a cocktail party if not an ice-breaking ritual among strangers? Bars have several characteristics that aid their clientele in executing the ritual of drunken debauchery. Here are some of them. The bar is kept darkened to help obscure less-than-perfect physical features. The dim lighting also encourages a relaxed atmosphere. The loud music encourages people to move in closer to one another in order to engage in lively conversation. Once bodies and minds are relaxed, meaningful (or meaningless) communication is facilitated.

My initial drug phase was inaugurated in a very posh house off Mulholland Drive. The owner was a music producer who maintained an assortment of instruments throughout his place. At certain local bars he was known for inviting only a select few over to engage in jam sessions and casual drug use. Making impromptu music and getting high with strangers was his own special ritual. This prestigious invite was extended to me only because of Dana's charm and wit.

At any rate, our host offered up his bar and personal stash to all his invitees. I made it known early on that my experience with drugs was practically nil. Even so, our host was more than willing to serve as my personal tutor. The options on the table were either coke or pot. I opted for the coke just to see what all the hype was about. And because cocaine was virgin territory for me, I asked a slew of questions and received an answer to each one. Respect for the drug was the sermon he was preaching, so it was never forced upon me. On the contrary, he asked that this choice be a strictly voluntary one on my part. Indeed it was.

So with my verbal concurrence and a hearty handshake, my lesson began. "Mulholland" showed me everything from proper bill roll technique to cutting and setting up a line suitable for a newbie such as myself. My first and only line that night could in no way rival Tony Montana's infamous mound-o-coke from the movie, *Scarface*. But it was enough to get the general feel for it. When the drug's effects began to take hold, he helped guide me through the experience. This thoughtful guidance certainly helped ease any hesitancy on my part.

The experience did not bring me to any sort of vision or realization. Instead, if there's a drug that can really amp one's ego off the charts, coke was it. Now if one is attempting to come to spiritual enlightenment, over-inflating the ego isn't the best way to go about it. According to Isaac Newton, what goes up must come down. And because the first half of my experience with coke took me to extraordinary heights, it was only a matter of time before the fall to unfathomable depths would set in. It soon became evident that this rich man's drug just wasn't going to be my thing.

Since I moved from Texas, the theme of my life was about trying new things and challenging old boundaries. If one drug wasn't my cup of tea, there was no reason to pull the emergency brake on the experimentation train just yet. I soon discovered pot was more my speed. In fact, my first transcendent experience resulted from a ritual involving the use of marijuana. What it offered me was a stilling of the mind. As a result, I felt as though my internal floodgates had been flung wide open. This experience led to numerous insights about myself and the world. I credit the use of a sound ritual for short-circuiting the urge to abuse marijuana in excess.

Learning to control my usage was the result of a chance meeting with a woman I met while donating blood in an American Red Cross bus. After failing to nail yet another audition, I stepped outside the studio to find that big red and white bus parked along the sidewalk. For some reason, donating blood seemed like the virtuous thing to do that day. And at the rate my acting career was going, Hollywood would suck the life out of me faster than the Red Cross ever could. Why not give my lifeblood to a worthier cause? Besides, my mom always professed that as one gives, so shall he receive.

After a nurse prepped my arm for the big prick to come, a woman seated across from me was already hooked up to an IV. She casually began conversing with me. When asked what I did for a living, I replied, "Jack of all trades but master of none." I added that working as a handyman paid the bills whenever acting couldn't. This friendly exchange was a welcome gesture that helped distract me from fact that a huge needle was already piercing my arm. I learned that she hailed from Jamaica, worked as a line producer for a famous reality TV show, and loved Bob Marley. Over time, she had even managed to suppress that distinct Jamaican accent. After the nurse had harvested a full bag of blood from each of us, we were rewarded with the customary cookie and punch. Before parting ways she offered her contact information and suggested we grab drinks sometime.

A few nights later, my new friend called me to ask if I would assist her with a project she had lying around her apartment. As a youth, I had sworn an oath with the Boy Scouts of America to always be of service, so naturally her proposal couldn't be refused. It soon became apparent that the hands-on experience she was seeking involved some craftiness in between the sheets. I was essentially seduced with a homemade meal and a joint for dessert. The music we swayed to that night was from Bob Marley's Greatest Hits album.

Could this be love? Not in the least. We just found ourselves routinely seeking solace in one another's company on lonely nights. And because our friendship was open-ended from the start, jealousy never reared its ugly head in our dating ritual. Eventually, she began instructing me on the art of pacing my drags and even discerning between the two strains of marijuana; *indica* and *sativa*. One strain fosters a mellow high while the other evokes a more euphoric experience. And though this smoking phase didn't conjure up any sort of spiritual insights, it definitely inspired some invigorating conversations. In essence, our friendship was an informal romance between two Los Angelinos that was bound by blood, so to speak.

At one point, she even suggested that I become her friend's escort for a night. This friend was hosting her own exclusive (invitation only) birthday party and wanted some arm candy. She also happened to be an extremely successful entrepreneur. We were introduced prior to the event to ensure a good fit, personality-wise. As it turned out, my date-to-be was a stunning older vixen who took an immediate liking to me.

On the evening of the illustrious affair, I arrived at my date's door where she greeted me ever so graciously. While she was giving me the five-cent tour, I could see that no expense had been spared. The entire event was catered which included two bartenders and three servers who liberally passed out hors d'oeuvres. The table at the entry of the living room had a large silver tray laden with joints for any guest to partake of. Even a psychic was hired to give free readings. The guest list was made up of a who's who in the interior design world, meaning that I wasn't going to know a soul there.

One couple in particular stood out from the rest due to their striking features. My mind led me to believe that they had little, if anything, to do with interior design. He had the whole Fabio thing going on and she was a jaw-dropping, double E 'd, platinum blonde knockout. She wore a red spaghetti-strapped dress that looked like it was painted on. When I was formally introduced, these two were very candid about their careers. They were porn stars. As if this gathering wasn't already spectacular.

Following a delicious sit-down dinner, everyone gathered in the living room which just had the feeling of the most inviting space to converse, drink and get high. Talk about sanctuaries! The walls were adorned with ornate pieces of art and collectibles from around the world and the furniture was mostly extravagant antiques. As the party progressed into the night, our host felt confident enough to kick her little soiree up a notch. An evening that started off with cocktails and pot smoking was now giving way to the cocaine finale. It's as if the first two drugs had been used to ease the transition to the high-octane stuff. Otherwise, everyone might have prematurely fallen off the deep end.

Many of my realizations about life have occurred in almost the same fashion. The religious, spiritual or practical events of my journey were always ancillary to something grander. It's as though the energies that governed my voyage purposely guided me toward trials that would result in crucial insights. The progression toward understanding was typically slow and steady, but that relaxed pace also made new realities far easier to assimilate. Otherwise, I might have gone mad years ago.

One of the trials I would face on the eve of that party was merely a prelude to a rude and long-overdue awakening - interpreting love and friendship anew. That night my host led me to her bedroom where we proceeded to make the double-backed monster. On a side note, her bed was the most comfortable surface I ever had the pleasure of being pleasured upon. But I had the surprise of my life immediately after sex when I was peremptorily given my marching orders. Apparently she wasn't the type to engage in gentle pillow talk.

Before this rather shameful experience, it was I who gently encouraged several ladies to take that dreaded walk of shame. My emotional detachment resulted from having my own heart tap danced upon one too many times. And being in the driver's seat of a relationship had an irresistible appeal. Yet there I was in unfamiliar territory, beaten at my own game. I was a king one moment and a pauper the next. I thought to myself, "How could someone be so dismissive?" But it was finally obvious. I had fallen prey to a bona fide man-eater. The tide had shifted and I could do nothing but embark on my own walk of shame.

As it turns out, I had been purposely led into the den of the lioness by my ex-part-time lover. Earlier in the affair she cautioned how our meaningless sexcapades were becoming tiresome and if I wanted to carry on this way, it would have to be without her. But as a gesture of her good intentions, she hooked me up with another like-minded individual. Generous though she was to do so, I still couldn't wrap my head around her willingness to give up obligation-free sex. Life was so much simpler without all of those sticky strings attached to it. But to her, those strings held the key to bonding with life on a much more meaningful level. That profound realization was all it took for her to permanently retire her booty call availability.

In no way did I regret her methodology. After all, life lessons learned the hard way tend to stick with me better than the ones I've simply heard from the lips of sages. Like it or not, the experience of being summarily dismissed from that bedroom ignited the desire to connect with a girl on a deeper level without the insincere gamesmanship. And while this notion didn't immediately put a stop to all of my shenanigans, it did get me to thinking, "How can I break free from this vortex of disappointment and shame?" Then, along came Katie.

Katie was the embodiment of a cool, calm and collected bad ass. We met by chance through a mutual friend at a local bar. Her ability to carry on a conversation about anything with anyone impressed me so because she didn't have to shift into character to do it. I had always relied on my chameleon-like persona to win over strangers. But not her. What you saw was what you got. She also spoke her mind without compromise or hesitation. I, on the other hand, made a habit of allowing small irritations to mount before finally blowing my top, usually resulting in an irrational, argumentative tantrum. I imagined that I could overcome some of my insecurities with her as a model.

Since genuine friendship was the only thing Katie ever offered me, I thought it foolish not to explore this relationship further. Who wouldn't want a sincere friend to explore this life with? Unfortunately, my cold and clichéd attitude toward women hadn't yet run its course. I could still sense my ego's reluctance to abandon its old ways and embrace the virtues of compassion and understanding. At the time I was unaware these qualities even existed between friends. But my flawed conception of friendship would soon expose me as an actual foe. But if experience has taught me anything, it would be this: Every sinner has a future and every saint has a past.

Before Katie I had tended to avoid people of a certain caliber, particularly anyone who was forthright, honest and/or capable of sniffing out my weaknesses. It was far easier to surround myself with women who just wanted me for my body. But there was something about my new friend that I just couldn't resist. Her physical beauty may have also influenced my decision to establish a relationship with someone so unlike my usual casual physical conquests. It was only a matter of time before I would crave something more than just friendship. But winning her heart would require real cunning and determination. And so began my campaign of what I perceived as selfless acts of kindness that included anything from weekly car washes to remodeling her entire bed and bath from the floor on up.

But Katie wouldn't budge. According to her, jumping headlong into a relationship would only compromise the friendship that she so thoroughly enjoyed building with me. It wasn't that she hadn't entertained the idea of something more; the timing was just off. She admitted to sensing something truly special about me even when we first met. It was just hard to pinpoint. The one conclusion she had no problem reaching was that I still needed some refining to smooth out all my rough inner and outer edges. Giving in to my single-minded aspiration to make her my romantic conquest would only stifle my progress toward self-improvement.

She just saw love in a totally different light than did I. In her view, truly loving someone was like herding a tortoise; it simply couldn't be rushed. Yet all I continued to focus on was what I couldn't have rather than appreciate the blessing of a sincere friend. Once my focus shifted from sidekick to suitor, the entire picture became severely distorted. Not only could I not accept "No" for an answer, I was even willing to discard our association altogether. How could she fail to succumb to my manifold charms? Why didn't she appreciate the many things I did for her? One day I was like, "What the hell, man!"

Katie finally decided it was high time I got a good talking to. She sat me down one day and said, "You're not in love; you only think you are. Have you ever taken time out to really get to know yourself or what you're capable of? If not, I highly recommend that you do. Otherwise, more of the same frustrations will just keep showing up in your life. Don't be afraid to put some distance between us either. Go out and travel the world or commit yourself to an adventure. Just stop postponing the life that is already patiently waiting for you. As for everything you've done for me, I never asked for any of it! That was all you. All of those things should have been done only because you wanted to do them. Despite it all, I am in no way obligated to give you anything in return. Now if you can come back to me at the end of all your explorations and profess that you're still in love, then there might be a chance for us."

At that point I had heard enough and just walked away. Still, something she said puzzled me. I should only do something for someone else because I want to? Being raised in a series of houses that weren't my own had committed me to a life of indentured servitude. Whenever someone would make an anonymous phone call to Child Protective Services to report my mother for negligence, the state would place me in the children's shelter. While there, I was expected to follow a set of rules that were enforced by total strangers. And since these individuals provided me with food, clothing and a warm bed, I felt compelled to obey.

When I was placed in foster care, a diabolical teenager got away with molesting me because of my perceived obligation to comply. I was just happy to get the essentials, no matter where they came from. And although he was the closest person I had to a father figure, Manuel still expected to be compensated for taking me in. The more he provided for me, the further indebted I became. Then my mother, the grand master of them all, used fear, guilt and shame to absolutely bend me to her will. Besides, how could I resist the person responsible for giving me life?

No wonder the majority of my friendships were destined to fail. I didn't see the world as it was, but through my own distorted prism. By projecting the template of my past broken relationships onto my new ones, the likelihood of failure was a near certainty. The problem was so obvious. When others didn't repay my acts of kindness in equal or greater measure, I would resort to using guilt or shame to force it out of them, just as was done unto me. Even worse, I managed to sabotage relationships in very much the same way my mother had. She rejected or was abusive to anyone who attempted to shed some light over her darkness. A victim identity had been established for my own personality long ago. How could I possibly act selflessly when so many had predisposed me to a warped sense of endless mutual obligation?

Now, when it came to my sex life, I pretty much called all the shots. Why? Because my mother never talked to me about it and without any parental pattern to follow or obey, I could shape that dimension of my life in whatever way I saw fit. It's also quite possible that my father influenced some of my sexual eccentricity. Almost every time I came over to visit he would be shacked up with a different woman. In his defense, he was a professional musician. And unlike my mother, he allowed me to watch cable TV while he was out playing a gig. Between his gigolo exhibitionism and the skinemax channel, I stood very little chance of becoming a one-woman type kind of guy.

Maybe Katie refused to take me seriously because I could conceivably leave her alone and brokenhearted down the road. Yet, despite our affinity, she summoned the courage to set me free. Her selfless act somehow sparked my own courage to journey beyond the realm of the familiar. To facilitate the process, I began ridding myself of all things Katie. Every picture or piece of memorabilia that we ever exchanged was tossed into the fireplace and set ablaze. This almost ritualistic rebirth might have been a bit rash, but it appeared to help because shortly thereafter a new chapter of my life started to unfold. A recent job change required me to leave Los Angeles and relocate to Hawaii. The threshold I had only dreamt of crossing one day had actually materialized.

Co-dependent relationships shackled me to the dogmas I was so desperately trying to escape. Yet I had been given a shot at a fresh start, one that could potentially put my masquerading persona to rest for good. Besides, what was the worst that could happen if I just stopped trying to please everyone all the time? It seemed to be working for Katie because she couldn't care less what others thought of her. When we first met, she immediately put the ball in my court by giving me the choice to either accept or reject her at face value. I, on the other hand, made a habit of putting the needs of others ahead of my own to earn their approval. Then, whenever I felt entitled to a bit of restitution, they would all feed me a similar line, "I never asked you for anything. You just took it upon yourself to give." Ultimately, they were in the right for casting doubt over my intentions because if I wasn't acting selflessly, what was my real agenda?

And while the world may not have owed me anything, I definitely owed it to myself to begin cultivating harmonious relationships without burdening others with my own dubious moral imperative. Moreover, what was the point of leaving Texas if I was just going to continue along the same path? Reinventing myself would require establishing a new set of rules to replace the severely distorted ones. That didn't necessarily mean dismissing everything my mom had taught me. If any of her principles represented basic human decency or benefited humanity in some way, throwing them out would be counterproductive. But obeying a social rule because it was demanded of me just wasn't going to cut it anymore.

Poet Khalil Gibran once wrote, "If it is the despot you would dethrone, see first that his throne erected within is destroyed." Though I may have left my mother behind in Texas, her early training was still governing me from within. The only way to rid myself of that negative influence would be to upgrade her beliefs with new experiences. Only which persona would be best suited to handle this essential transformation? My chameleon facade always managed to keep me out of trouble by adapting itself to practically any situation. However, Hawaii felt like the perfect place to develop a completely new persona, one fully vested in satisfying its own needs first. Who would know the difference anyway? All my old friends and acquaintances who could testify to the contrary would be on the mainland.

This new persona would make no apologies for who he was or what he wanted. Every other aspect of my identity would be built upon that sole conviction. The final step involved putting new ideas in place to support that belief. The way I see it, ideas and beliefs work in tandem to support general points of view. I liken a belief to a tabletop and individual ideas as the legs supporting it. Without all four legs in place, the tabletop would be rendered unstable and could possibly collapse. Therefore, when it comes to changing a belief I first determine the underlying ideas that give a particular point of view credence. Once they've been identified, I can then substitute old ideas with new ones until the belief itself has changed.

For example, the old me believed that lending assistance to another automatically indebted them to return the favor. The ideas that supported this belief included a history of being beholden to others in exchange for the essentials of life, fear of what might happen should I fail to comply, or experiencing guilt as a means of coercion and the shame that was felt for having to submit to these conditions. But thanks to the guidance of a few key mentors, I finally felt empowered to alter my destiny. The only drawback to this new sense of entitlement was the overwhelming temptation to take it to the extreme.

Not only did I believe myself to be in total control this time around, but the ideas supporting this notion would inevitably condemn me to repeat a failed story - namely my mother's. One of her personalities put me and countless others through hell because it understood nothing of accountability, nor was it patient, cooperative or remorseful. It only knew how to create chaos. And to what end? To prove itself right by making everyone else wrong? It found itself condemned to a life of solitude as a result. As the only person left behind in her immediate circle, I was subjected to a relentless barrage of torment and abuse. After all, misery loves her company.

The trial run for my experimental personality began the moment I relocated to Hawaii. As an added incentive, my new boss had recently shared his philosophy for personal success with me. He said, "It's better to ask for forgiveness than for permission." That was just the encouragement I needed to proceed accordingly. The results spoke for themselves. I was able to get everything I wanted from anyone I needed it from. With respect to my job, I had to be this way to fulfill the expectations of a merciless employer. The women I started dating, on the other hand, didn't deserve to be treated with so little regard. But as my mom always said, "Go to bed with dogs, wake up with fleas." Not caring just came with the territory and the less attentive I became, the more they tried to change me. The awakening of my inner bad boy was inevitable.

Another classic sequence in Joseph Campbell's *Monomyth* is called *The Meeting with the Goddess.* It represents what is known as the *hieros gamos,* or sacred marriage. This is where the hero experiences a powerful and all-encompassing love that is symbolized by a union of opposites which is not necessarily a marriage. This union can develop internally when the hero begins to see himself in a non-dualistic way. This is also when the hero tends to find another person for whom he or she has complete and selfless love. While this meeting doesn't have to involve a woman, that was not to be the case with me.

Fate would align me with another independent and courageous soul. But unlike Katie, I never imagined we could become so much more. That *knowing* sensation that Betsy warned of wasn't even remotely close to awakening within me just yet. In fact, it took almost losing this person for me to finally recognize the obvious. Many of the individuals who fostered my personal growth were found right at my doorstep, but it wasn't until I felt an overwhelming desire for change that I could identify them. And how would I ever notice the significance of this person when I was so completely fixated on my goal of personal fulfillment? Experience would prove that love always finds a way.

This little island angel was unlike any of the toxic fare I had grown accustomed to dating. That was probably why all hell broke loose early on in our relationship. She constantly challenged me to become better than I already thought myself to be. She reminded me of the self I once admired. As an eager-to-please optimist, I always strived to illustrate the positive aspects of life to please my mother's most critical personalities. But, time and again, my best efforts were met with even more brutality. Somewhere in the midst of it all I recalled reaching a tipping point where it felt there was nothing left to give. That sense of despair is what prompted my search for a way out. Otherwise, I could have easily sealed my fate without the possibility of escape.

But why was I rebelling so fiercely against this darling person? Thanks to her tenacity, the answer was soon apparent. As the one who was responsible for resolving all the issues within the household, I grew to appreciate the chaos around me which gave me a sense of purpose and fulfillment. But once I had resolved the largest issue by moving out, I unconsciously began looking for new drama to resolve, even if it meant pulling it out of thin air. Experience has also shown that if someone searches for new ways to become offended, this world won't disappoint.

All it took to reactivate the chaos, this time self-generated, was to allow someone into my life who emanated peace.

The old patterns that had governed me for so long clearly would not die easily. And I wasn't even consciously orchestrating this turmoil. It arose from habits and patterns formed in the past, based on a warped world view imposed on me by others. While the role of savior to someone else had been beneficial at one time, the habits formed by that role had become a negative influence. I had been transformed from savior into one needing to be saved.

Still, for all the grief I caused this new girl, she could only think to repay my shortsightedness with more kindness. At first it seemed as though I had met my opposite. She could hardly conceive of the tragedies that had befallen me so early in life because, in comparison, her life seemed so normal. Nonetheless, there was nothing she wouldn't have done for me. Unfortunately, I was too busy being my own person, and in doing so, completely disregarded the virtues my mother had taught me. By tossing the baby out with the bathwater, the good with the bad from my mother, there was no limit to my self-absorption. But as I soon discovered, even angels have a breaking point.

Her eagerness to please eventually dissolved into total disinterest. In actuality, she felt more disappointed with herself than with me. After all, I was just being myself (or so she was led to believe), whereas she felt she should have known better. The only mystery was why she had let it go on for so long. Ironically, she too had grown accustomed to keeping men at a distance. Her life was far less complicated without sticky romantic entanglements. Yet, like Katie, she admitted sensing something different about me that compelled her to give me more of a chance than she might have otherwise. Also, having never before had her heart broken, she thought, "What better time than now?" This young paragon of virtue was truly a gift from the Universe, or Heaven, or whatever place is charged with dream fulfillment.

At the risk of losing her for good, I finally relented. It's somewhat paradoxical, but allowing myself to become vulnerable again reacquainted me with that veiled passion that makes dramatic transitions appear seamless. This tenacious, blonde windfall was an effective communicator and was willing to share her useful insights, provided that I first listen to her call me out on all my bullshit. Her revelations really hit home for me. The level of understanding and self-awareness I finally achieved was stunning.

As she expressed her viewpoints, I would experience a flashback to the instance in question. In every case it was clear that egocentricity got the better of me. Strangely, during each of these illustrations it felt as though her emotional state merged with mine, setting off an avalanche of raw emotion. All I could do was bury my head in my hands and sob uncontrollably. Was this really how it was for others dealing with my baggage? All this time I had been acting out like an angry child unable to express himself verbally. So I dished out blame and recriminations while avoiding the true nature of my angst.

Recognizing how I truly wanted to turn things around, this godsend of a girl taught me how to express myself without entangling myself in a web of confusion. Like Mr. X, she emphasized the importance of staying on point rather than lunging straight for the jugular. Write down my feelings first, then shuffle through them to find a reoccurring theme. From that pattern I should be able to narrow down a single concern. To resolve the issue, it might prove helpful to present my concern as a thoughtful question rather than as an attack which would only raise the other person's defenses. Also, I should keep in mind that each person's perspective is open to interpretation, so if more clarity is needed, just ask. What a stark departure from how I learned to communicate with my mother.

I recalled something from *The Power of Myth* series that gradually added an intriguing depth to all of my supposed mistakes. Joseph Campbell paraphrased the German philosopher, Schopenhauer, on the subject of will. Essentially he said that when you look back over your life it seems to have had an order to it, as if composed by someone. Even those events that seemed merely accidental turned out to be essential components in a consistent plot. Just as your dreams are composed by an aspect of yourself of which your consciousness is unaware, so your entire life has been orchestrated by the will within you. Just as the people you've met by chance affected the structuring of your life, so you have in turn affected other lives and the whole thing meshes together like a big symphony.

For a time I had believed that true strength came from being static and unmovable. However, I came to realize that my chameleon-like behavior was, in its own way, an expression of power. Sacrificing my ego allowed me to find common ground with others. Having the strength to admit my weaknesses to myself also took an act of courage, one that could not have been possible while maintaining a fixed attitude. My unyielding persona may have made life convenient at one time, but only because it didn't require anything more than what I was willing to give. However, opening the heart to allow love to flow in both directions called for a totally new approach, one that would only work if discovered in tandem with another. Experience had finally taught me that in order to develop meaningful harmony with the world, I would first have to establish symmetry from within.

EPILOGUE:

To Know Nothing

Attempting to master the inner dimension has resulted in a truly transcendent experience that has helped me overcome the fear of change while granting me the freedom to live my life. Still, I could have never made it this far without the help of some very crafty adversaries. Not only did these spectacular individuals mentor me, but I have also had the good fortune to have been their friend. Whilst sitting here, typing out the remaining words to this epic and wondrous story of mine, I feel eternal gratitude for meeting such _____ along the way. What they are to me is truly beyond words.

Since I began writing this book in October of 2009, much has changed. JoAnn has since married a good guy who adores her. The two of them share a loving home with their two dogs. Though she hasn't begun teaching yet, all of her credentials are in order and it is only a matter of time now. After being apart for nearly twelve years, we recently took the opportunity to catch up and we both agreed that neither one of us had any regrets about sharing a small portion of our lives together. Perhaps the things that are so good in our lives now could have only come to us through a series of trials and revelations. We've certainly have had our share. We still remain good friends.

Max and I spoke a few months before I completed the first draft of this book. He was the same old nuisance that I knew back when but ever proud of me still. After attempting to reach him recently, I was only able to get a recording that stated his line had been disconnected. Something tells me that his phone line wasn't the only thing that has since been disengaged. After all, he wasn't in the best of shape last we spoke. Furthermore, nothing in this life truly surprised him anymore, leading me to believe that he was ready for another show. Regardless, the guidance he bestowed upon me remains eternally alive through this literary work. Because if there was one person who believed I could pull it off from the start, it was Max.

Dennis remains in Burbank, California. Unfortunately, he recently brought it to my attention that he has had Parkinson's since prior to the day we first met. The symptoms just weren't as prevalent back then. I wish that there were more I could do for him. What I have managed to do is assure him that I always enjoyed his company and truly appreciated the wealth of words he bestowed upon my tiny brain.

As for the ringmaster herself, we still keep in touch. My mother has since had to leave Rice Road because it became entirely too difficult for her to handle alone and now resides in a nursing home. It's been nearly two years since we last saw each other. Even so, we talk at least once a week, and the conversations seem to get more meaningful each time. It is now becoming apparent that her memory isn't what it once was. However, the nursing home staff has informed me that she still appears to experience personality switches, though to a lesser degree. Nonetheless, I will always have eternal gratitude for having been raised by the many faces of a dynamic woman whom I'm forever proud to call Mom.

Up to this point, my journey has taken me from one extreme to another and back again. Thanks to the guidance I've received along the way, many of the flawed character traits that once weighed so heavily upon me have vanished. It seems at times that the person I described in these pages was a total stranger to me. Even so, I wrote this book with the intent of helping others and in doing so, improved upon the whole of my life. While piecing together this book, I would sometimes light a few candles to help establish a peaceful ambiance in the room. The metaphor of one candle lighting many without ever dimming itself captures the essence of what I was trying to accomplish.

I predict that humanity might, one day, witness the death of divided nations and the rebirth of a single country called Earth where we, as brothers and sisters from all four corners, can celebrate it as one. Perhaps a simple shift in human consciousness is all that is required to bring such a grand dream to fruition. After all, perception is reality. In one of the interviews from The Power of Myth series, Joseph Campbell quotes a letter (written by Chief Seattle in 1852) which beautifully illustrates how the Native Americans perceived their world and all life in it. It reads as follows:

The President in Washington sends word that he wishes to buy our land. But how can you buy or sell the sky? The land? The idea is strange to us.

Every part of this earth is sacred to my people. Every shining pine needle, every sandy shore, every mist in the dark woods, every meadow - all are holy in the memory and experience of my people.

We're part of the earth and it is part of us. The perfumed flowers are our sisters. The bear, the deer, the great eagle, these are our brothers.

Each ghostly reflection in the clear water of the lakes tells of events and memories in the life of my people. The water's murmur is the voice of my father's father.

The rivers are our brothers. They carry our canoes and feed our children.

If we sell you our land, remember that the air is precious to us, that the air shares its spirit with all the life it supports. The wind that gave our grandfather his first breath also receives his last sigh.

This we know: the earth does not belong to man, man belongs to the earth. All things are connected like the blood that unites us all. Man did not weave the web of life, he is merely a strand in it. Whatever he does to the web, he does to himself.

Your destiny is a mystery to us. What will happen when the buffalo are all slaughtered? What will happen when the secret corners of the forest are heavy with the scent of many men and the view of the ripe hills is blotted by talking wires? The end of living and the beginning of survival.

When the last red man has vanished with his wilderness, and his memory is only the shadow of a cloud moving across the prairie, will these shores and forests still be here? Will there be any of the spirit of my people left?

We love this earth as a newborn loves its mother's heartbeat. So, if we sell you our land, love it as we have loved it. Care for it, as we've cared for it. Hold in your mind the memory of the land as it is when you receive it. Preserve the land for all children, and love it, as God loves us all.

One thing we know - there is only one God. No man, be he Red man or White man, can be apart. We are brothers after all.

Tolstoy once remarked, "Everyone talks about changing the world but no one starts by changing himself." It's as though humanity has been conditioned to dwell in a system that purposely depletes one's desire to take risks in order to find life. The remedy for curing that lack of confidence in my own life came about by realizing that I am a spirit having a human experience and not the other way around. I've since learned to live on purpose by embracing the experience of being human. Sacrificing my idle time to write this book has given me a glimpse of what it's like to be truly alive.

Sacrificing one's self for a greater purpose can be likened to how a sperm cell willingly sacrifices itself to achieve the aim of fertilizing an egg. Still, out of death comes life as the egg begins to transform into an embryo. That embryo then undergoes several more divisions before finally mutating into an infant. That infant then continues to grow outside the womb, learning from and influencing others as it traverses through life. Then the developing child eventually becomes a parent charged with protecting and sacrificing for the life that it brings forth. Similarly, trees bear fruit that contains seeds which carry the promise of future trees.

I used to wonder what my place was in this infinite cycle. What, if anything, was I sacrificing myself for? For the most part, I was only interested in doing the things that everyone else was doing. Yet that too turned into a vicious cycle. In order to break the cycle, I first needed to identify with something greater than or other than myself. The first step involved realizing what my natural talent could be and then ordering myself around it.

One can discover a wealth of wisdom simply by carefully examining the most mundane things. Take the ceramic cup that cradles my morning cup of coffee for instance. In order for the clay to harden, it must first be heated in the controlled inferno of a potter's kiln. Cooler temperatures can't elicit the useful qualities from the clay that intense heat can. So the next time someone gets you fired up, recognize that an opportunity has arisen to draw forth latent qualities in both yourself and your opponent. After all, tensions are the source of energies that can serve to generate new and exciting ideas.

Ideas are like blooming roses, ever opening unto the light. The old blooms must fall away so new ones can spring to life. Similarly, every idea is a working hypothesis. My mentors have always encouraged me to challenge old ideas as well as beliefs. If a computer is to run optimally, its software must be updated continually. Similarly, I too must continue to ask myself, "Are the beliefs I cling to relevant to this moment?"

I'm a big believer in the idea of Karma. It's a force that doesn't seem to be bound by the parameters of good and evil. You reap what you sow. Whatever I've cast out into the world has always found its way back to me in one way or another, especially my less than admirable choices. Decisions and choices aren't necessarily the same thing. Today's decisions are derived from yesterday's choices. Choices provide us with feedback, out of which informed decisions can then be established.

Remaining centered between the temporal apparitions of good and evil has become an ongoing practice in my life. This slant gives me the opportunity to refrain from labeling circumstances as either good or bad. Besides, who can honestly tell one from the other. I'm certain many of the things I've done in the past were evil for some as they were positive for others. However, experience has repeatedly demonstrated that my failures were nothing more than future successes in their infancy. I can also attest that success isn't as sweet unless it follows several bitter defeats. Refraining from making premature value judgments allows me to see more clearly the hidden value in all things.

Max would always tell me that the road to hell is paved with good intentions because he recognized that every act generates unintended consequences. Even leaning toward the light can have negative effects. That is why the path to enlightenment is often compared to the narrow edge of a razor. Only few actually muster the courage to steady themselves between abandoning the familiarity of the way things were done before and conquering the fear associated with exploring the unknown. I have frequently seen how the world opens up for those who've managed to find a central purpose in their lives. Despite personal danger, Gandhi imposed change on the world by setting out to better understand the opposition, not conquer it by force. Creating change by peaceful means became his legacy. What legacy will your own endeavors leave behind?

Scientists are on a quest to find answers for every question the human mind can devise. Their goal isn't just to discover the source of life, but to unravel its meaning. Does life really have any meaning? Who knows. What I can say is that affirming the mystery of life has been my most visceral experience to date. Am I concerned whether my life really means anything? Not particularly. Because for me, life isn't so much about knowledge but rather the richness I've gained from personal experience. After all, the world that once belonged to my ancestors is not the world of today. Often, the vices of today become the virtues of tomorrow. Morals and morality vary from place to place and are constantly changing. Perhaps the most sensible way to live your life is to actively experience its radiance in all things. The only thing I'm absolutely sure of is that there are no absolutes.

Embarking on the inward quest has become the Holy Grail of my journey. Though some might think that finding the grail should be the goal of the quest, I have managed to achieve relief from suffering by recognizing that the Holy Grail isn't something to be obtained physically; it need only be realized spiritually. Inner exploration is what initially spurred my desire to achieve higher aims for my personal development. Sharing those boons with the masses is just an added bonus. One journey to the bottom of the sea could never account for all its mysteries. Likewise, my journey inward probably didn't conjure up every single demon, but it was one hell of a good start. Even if some of those demons couldn't be defeated, they were at least relegated to their proper place in my life.

I thought I knew by age twenty-five exactly how my life would play out. Like a cup that was already full, there seemed room for no other possibilities. As a result, my expectations were accompanied by loads of frustration until I eventually learned to toss out ideas that no longer served any useful purpose. Even the U.S. Constitution has provisions engineered into its framework that warrant defense against foreign enemies as well as domestic. We the people are both the creators and protectors of our own freedoms. Similarly, what we think about most often can serve as a guide for determining the course of our destiny. As I can attest from personal experience, thoughts can liberate as well as enslave.

A friend who once served in the Peace Corps shared an insight that he gained during his service. He was assigned the task of teaching the natives of a small rural community to properly sow corn crops. Because they had always planted their crops in rows running up and down a hillside, most of the seeds were washed away by heavy rains. The seeds were also spaced inconsistently, causing the plants to clump too closely together.

The problem was easily remedied by shifting the rows from a vertical alignment to one that followed the horizontal line of the hill. He also instructed them to allow the weeds to grow so that the roots would help hold the dirt in place. Finally, small holes needed to be dug and evenly spaced along each row to receive the new seedlings. Previous experience assured him that this new configuration would protect the crop against the threat of a total washout. It wasn't an impossible task but it certainly demanded immediate attention due to the approaching rainy season.

After equipping the locals with a sound, proven method, it seemed that such logic would surely win the day, and indeed it did. Only it wasn't the sort of logic my friend was hoping for. After several months had passed he returned to participate in the harvest but was stunned to see that the crops were still planted in the same, sloppy configuration as before. Confused and annoyed, he asked why they had totally ignored his valuable advice. The response he got was surprising but understandable from their perspective. According to the locals, their method produced predictable results that they could rely on. None of them had any idea how much corn the foreigner's method would produce, so prudence dictated that they should stick with the old way.

From the natives' viewpoint, they could always estimate the size of their harvest based on the proven results from the old method, poor though they might be. Therefore, they saw no need to change their ways. In that moment, my friend recognized that his proposal posed a perceived threat to the very livelihood of the people he was attempting to help. His story contains the elements of three distinct realities - his, theirs and one profound truth. If you want to keep getting what you're getting, keep doing what you're doing. Finally, if courage is all you lack for moving ahead in life, heed the words of my mom who once told me, "A ship is safe in a harbor but that's not what ships are built for."